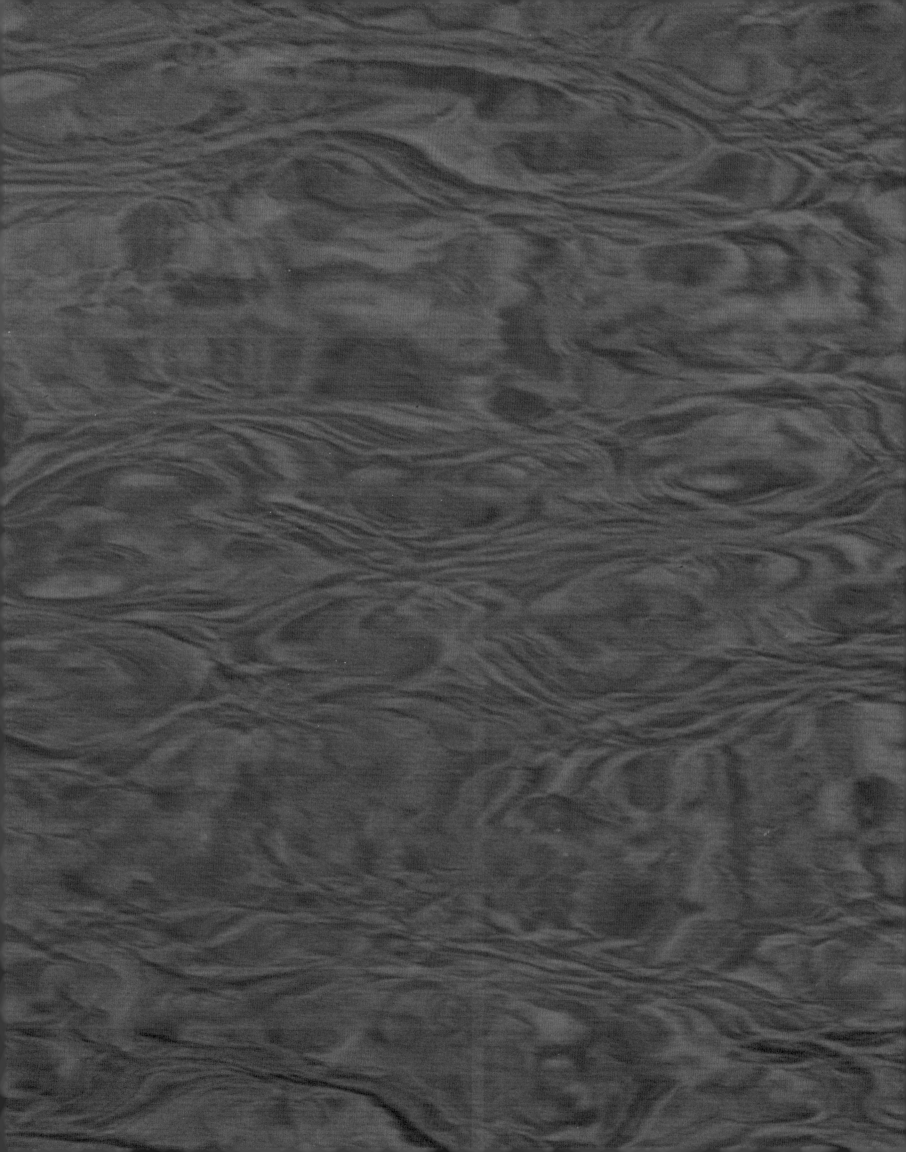

THE ATLANTIC
Salmon Fly

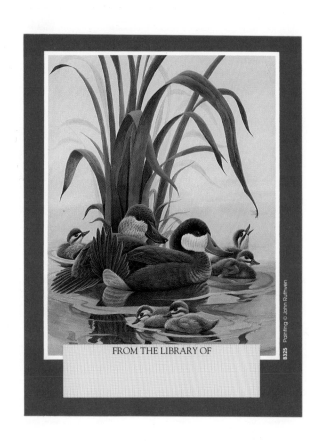

THE ATLANTIC
Salmon Fly

The Tyers
and
Their Art

Judith Dunham

PHOTOGRAPHS BY

John Clayton

CHRONICLE BOOKS · SAN FRANCISCO

ACKNOWLEDGMENTS

It has been a pleasure to work with Dennis Gallagher and John Sullivan, whose exceptional talents have resulted in such a handsomely and elegantly designed book. Photographer John Clayton has taken the extraordinary Atlantic salmon flies of twenty-three flytyers and given them beautiful settings and images, showing the flies as they have never been presented before in print.

Thanks also to Pam Richards for providing access to the collection of Joseph D. Bates, and to John Betts, Bill Cushner, Ted Niemeyer, Wayne Luallen, Alan Bramley, Jim Adams, Al Cohen, and Alec Jackson for their invaluable assistance.

Most of all, I am indebted to all of the flytyers in this book, who graciously allowed me to visit them and to talk with them about their lives and their work. I will always remember the experience.

— *Judith Dunham*

Art direction and design:
Dennis Gallagher and John Sullivan,
Visual Strategies, San Francisco
Photography and photo-styling: John Clayton
Copy editor: Christine Carswell

Set in Minion and Stone Sans
Printed in Japan

Library of Congress Cataloging-in Publication Data
Dunham, Judith
    The Atlantic salmon fly: the tyers and their art /
    Judith Dunham; photography by John Clayton.
        p. cm.
    Includes bibliographical references (p.).
    ISBN 0-87701-800-6 (cloth).
    1. Fly tying. 2. Fly tyers. 3. Flies, Artificial.
    4. Atlantic salmon fishing. I. Title.
    SH451.D86   1991
    688.7'912—dc20   90-22661
                                                CIP

Distributed in Canada by:
Raincoast Books
112 East Third Avenue
Vancouver, British Columbia
V5T 1C8

10 9 8 7 6 5 4 3 2 1

CHRONICLE BOOKS
275 Fifth Street
San Francisco, California 94103

FRONT COVER
Albert J. Cohen
Unnamed pattern from the 19th century

BACK COVER
Bob Veverka
(clockwise from top left)
Purple Ghost, Ghost, Double Ackroyd, Gardner

Contents

JUNGLE COCK

BLUE CHATTERER

INTRODUCTION

Judith Dunham

So graceful is the shape, so resplendent the palette and intricate the design, that the Atlantic salmon fly surely must have been invented for more than luring a fish. This precious object, though made of feathers, fur, and tinsel, looks finely painted or inlaid with gems. The hook initially seems like a concession to practicality, a simple armature bound with gold or silver and supporting a fetish that explodes with spears of color. Yet this curved piece of metal is an unmistakable reminder that the destiny of this bejeweled treasure is to be knotted at the end of a fishing line, cast out over a river, and allowed to sink to its fate beneath the flowing water. For the Atlantic salmon, known as the king of game fish, deserves to be enticed with the crown jewel of flies.

The quest for the Atlantic salmon, long regarded as a pursuit as noble as the quarry, has always carried a fitting sense of exclusivity. True to its name, the Atlantic salmon is sought in northerly waterways with access to the Atlantic Ocean. Journeying to the homelands of the salmon can be a costly and complicated excursion. Many of the rivers in Norway, Scotland, England, Ireland, Iceland, and the maritime provinces of Canada are privately owned and can be fished only by prior arrangement, and the angler who has secured an opening on a sought-after beat has paid dearly for the good fortune. In its elitism and expense, fly-fishing for the famed Atlantic salmon remains almost as rarefied today as it was in the era of the Victorian sports and ghillies, who in their reverence for the king of game fish, and for the ritual of its pursuit, refined the Atlantic salmon fly to an apogee of beauty and flamboyance.

Seeking out the Atlantic salmon in its fabled rivers and honoring it with a kind of talisman descended from the excessiveness of Victorian design may seem like a strangely cultish form of fishing. Although several flytyers in this book fish more than occasionally for salmon, few of them live within a convenient distance of an Atlantic salmon river. However infatuated they may be with fishing for salmon, they spend more of their time immersed in crafting a specific type of fishing fly that is appreciated today as much as a form of art as it is valued as an angling tool. Whereas the geographical territory of the Atlantic salmon is as circumscribed as it was at the

GOLD ROPE AROUND PASTEL FLOSS

GOLDEN PHEASANT TIPPETS

KENYA
CRESTED
GUINEA
FOWL

satisfaction of tying and fishing their own flies, they sought new ways to use their skills. They glimpsed such a challenge in the plates of an antique angling book, in a fly or two in the fly box of an angler who had fished in Canada or Scotland, or in those few instructional manuals that tantalized readers with directions for making a fly they had never seen before. Many other flies are esthetically rewarding to the eyes, demanding of the fingers, and even tempting to a fish. Yet when these flytyers discovered the Atlantic salmon fly, they were immediately enthralled with what has been lauded as the pinnacle of the craft of flytying, the zenith of the angling arts, the ultimate test of a flytyer's ability.

If the Atlantic salmon merits a fly of such artistry, one wonders why it must be a worthy fish. The world of nature abounds in tales of survival, but the story of the cyclic journeys of the Atlantic salmon transcends reality to become a parable of adversity, tenacity, and rebirth. Atlantic salmon, unlike most trout, spend their lives alternating between fresh and salt water. Leaving the rivers where they were born, they swim in the spring to the ocean. Those that have escaped the predators along the way remain at sea for a season or more to nourish themselves for the mission that lies ahead. Driven by a primordial impulse, most salmon return in autumn to the same rivers where they were born in order to spawn.

Dedicated to its journey upstream, the silvery fish called *Salmo salar*, the great leaper, may erupt above the surface of the water, without any apparent purpose. This leg of the odyssey is also cause for struggle. The effort made by the salmon to persist against the current, up waterfalls, and around rocks, culminating in the act of spawning, may leave it too weak and vulnerable to be able to return to the sea. But if the Atlantic salmon survives, it will live on, unlike the Pacific salmon, to

turn of the century, the domain of the Atlantic salmon fly reaches across the ocean for which it is named and far beyond the British Isles, the place of its origin. The revival of interest among flytyers, and as a result among collectors, has grown to such an extent over the last twenty years that people from Japan to Canada to Holland, and from California to Texas to Massachusetts, have been seduced by the beauty of this traditional fly and by the aura of mystique surrounding its legends and the prey that inspired its design.

This renaissance of the Atlantic salmon fly is in many ways an outgrowth of the increasing popularity of fly-fishing as a recreational sport. As beginning anglers learned to cast with a fly rod and acquired all the other skills needed to catch a fish, they naturally were curious and motivated to tie their own flies. Many books and magazines published during the 1960s and 1970s helped teach these neophytes about the behavior and food preferences of the trout, the most common quarry of the fly-fisher, and the techniques for tying the full range of appropriate artificial flies. As these legions of tyers became more confident about their abilities and enjoyed the

repeat the cycle. In their pilgrimage to their place of generation and regeneration, the salmon may be delayed by one impediment outside nature's scheme—the angler, who drifts through the water an ornate object on a hook.

For every angler throughout the centuries who has cast a line into a pool or run of a salmon river, there is an explanation for why the fish has taken, or not taken, a fly. Despite all the theories, anglers choose a fly knowing that, when Atlantic salmon embark on their purposeful migration up their native rivers, they have largely ceased to feed. Strategize as anglers and flytyers are compelled to do, they have never been able to conclude with confidence why a salmon responds to an artificial fly. The functional Atlantic salmon fly, therefore, need not look to the fish like a natural form of food that it once consumed. Nor need it be a rococo fantasy. Unpredictable in their preference for either, the salmon have unwittingly released the creativity of the flytyer, who is free to conceive of the simplest or most opulent abstraction imaginable.

Not all modern flytyers have opted to dress the splendorous flies once made by the Victorians to wile a salmon—or, as some surmise, to impress one another with their flytying ingenuity and angling prowess. When the Atlantic salmon fly made its transatlantic migration from Great Britain to Canada and the east coast of the United States, it left behind the Victorian proclivity for elaboration. The flytyers of the New World, motivated by necessity, developed simpler, more practical salmon fly patterns, replacing the intricately feathered wings with tufts of hair easily available from native game. Unusual feathers occasionally crept into a Canadian or American salmon fly, since flytyers could never resist the temptation to

dress up a fly, for themselves if not for the fish. The smaller, streamlined hair-wing flies, embellished with silver or gold tinsel or colored floss or dyed feathers, came to be preferred, by the mid-twentieth century, for Atlantic salmon fishing on both sides of the Atlantic.

For most contemporary flytyers, including those in this book, their interest in Atlantic salmon flies began less with an urge to fish for salmon than with an entrancing look at the rich colors and textures in a classic feather-wing fly. When flytyers remember why they wanted to make these lavish flies, their recollections inevitably lead to their desire for a challenge. Acquiring the skills to marry, or join, strips of feathers into an apparently solid wing, or to make smooth wraps of silk floss and uniformly spaced tinsel around the hook, demands considerable patience, dexterity, and practice. Reaching technical mastery, however, is only part of the task of being able to tie an artful fly. The other is finding the materials, a potentially obsessive pursuit that can easily be a hobby separate from the actual tying of the fly. Converted into avid feather collectors, flytyers become eager to find out what the actual birds look like and where they come from,

absorbing in the process a vocabulary sprinkled with taxo-
nomic classifications.

Just as a painter seeks the best pigments and canvas or a
sculptor the finest tools and stone, flytyers covet the most
exquisite substances. The airy pastel of toucan, the electric
blue of chatterer, the fiery orange of Indian crow, the illusory
iridescence of peafowl, the golden glimmer of pheasant
crest—this mosaic of exotic and unique plumage is so vibrant
that it makes an Atlantic salmon fly appear illuminated from
within. The need for such feathers as raw materials seems only
superficially to explain the compulsion to collect them. Like
the passion to own unique and priceless jewels, there is among
many Atlantic salmon fly tyers a desire to possess rare feathers,
a desire for ownership that seems to run deeper than the mere
accumulation of them as inventory. It is as if the feathers are
still imbued with the life force of the birds they once cloaked.
A stroke of speckled bustard, a dab of jungle cock, and a ges-
ture of toucan perpetuate the spirit and honor the beauty of
the once-living animal.

A century ago, such exotic feathers as well as furs, which
were coveted for fashion more than for flies, could be obtained
from the importers of specimens from Africa, South America,
and Asia. A very different climate faces the flytyer of the late
twentieth century—an era of shrinking natural resources, of
vanishing habitats and disappearing species. Flytyers can con-
veniently, and in good conscience, obtain such common
materials or by-products as the chicken hackle, deer and elk
hair, and duck and goose feathers that they need for trout,
bass, and saltwater flies. They have made ingenious use of
modern synthetic materials. But for Atlantic salmon fly tyers
wanting to copy or emulate the fly designs of the past, the rari-
ty that contributes to the appeal of these exotic feathers is the
very obstacle to procuring them.

GOLDEN PHEASANT CREST

EUROPEAN JAY

BRONZE MALLARD

After international trade in such avian specimens came under scrutiny at the turn of the last century, a series of acts and treaties has attempted to restrict the exportation of rare and endangered species from their native lands. Each year, species are eliminated from or added to the list of birds allowed to be imported, although the language of the regulations can be frustrating to interpret. Measured against the many threats to the environments of rare birds and mammals around the world, flytyers' desire for materials has a relatively insignificant impact. There is a growing sentiment, however, that any use of an exotic feather or fur, regardless of its legality, reinforces an attitude that condones the exploitation of nature. The logic behind this point of view is that tying flies with rare natural materials seems inconsistent with those principles in fly-fishing that aggressively advocate conservation of the fish and their habitat and prescribe that catch-and-release fishing be standard practice. The same ethics, it can be argued, should be extended beyond the protection of the salmon or trout alone into every facet of fly-fishing and its effect on the world that makes the sport possible.

Atlantic salmon fly tyers have a number of choices in addition to the legal purchase of imported materials from exotic species. Feathers dropped from birds in aviaries, zoos, and pet shops are sometimes available, and very effective alternates have been made by dyeing common feathers to simulate the more exotic ones. It would be easy to blame the Victorians and other fly dressers of the past who, unable to foresee the ramification of their passion for beautiful feathers, bequeathed to the flytying world hundreds of fly patterns whose dressings, or recipes, call for unusual plumage. The traditional salmon fly looks so premeditated in every aspect of its conception and execution that it seems governed by steadfast rules. Many of the earlier fly dressers were, like those of today, experimentors whose work ranged from incorporating a newly discovered material to developing a wholly different pattern. One only need look at the variations on the Dusty Miller in this book to see that, although they all have the same name, they look quite different. Despite the assertions of many flytyers and authors, the composition of the Atlantic salmon fly is not defined by absolutes. There is no correct or incorrect method, no right or wrong material, for tying a fly. If it is approached as a matrix for design, the Atlantic salmon fly is equally artful and distinctive whether expressed in so-called traditional materials or in paint or pencil on paper.

The appeal of re-creating a salmon fly pattern from the past and the desire to procure the same materials used by the early fly dressers are intrinsic to the nostalgia and romanticism that pervade the whole sport. Regardless of the modernization of tackle and the endless proliferation of theories, the angler of today, like all those who came before, still opens a fly box and selects an artificial fly to tempt a fish from the waters.

Each fly-fisher who steps into a stream to cast that fly performs against the backdrop of fly-fishing history with props handed down over decades of tradition. The Atlantic salmon fly especially is steeped in history. The essential form of the salmon fly and often the specific pattern from which it was tied connect the flytyer of the late twentieth century to the past, whether to the pre-Victorians or the Victorians, or to the early twentieth century pioneers of the Canadian and American traditions. Each fly is a descendant and an evocation of a particular time and place.

Nothing is so suggestive of the imagined romance and gentility of that earlier age than the very names of the flies. The Helmsdale Doctor, the Beauly Snow Fly, the Silver Test, and the Highland Gem call forth the storied rivers, firths, and lochs of Scotland and England. Little is known of the lives of the sports and ghillies who stood on a river's bank in Ireland or Wales a hundred years ago, but their names are immortalized along with the creations they invented in the hopes of calling a salmon from its waters. Who, the armchair time-traveler muses, were Sir Richard, Lady Caroline, and John Ferguson? The Black Prince and the Red King, the Purple Emperor and

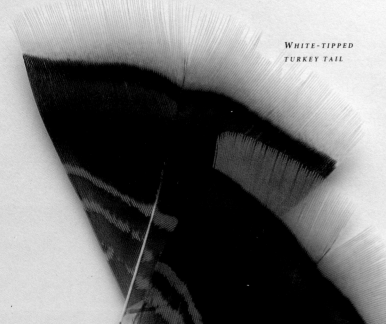

the Harlequin? What sublime visions were in the minds of nineteenth century fly dressers when they named their flies the Rosy Dawn and the Evening Star, the Thunder and Lightning and the Floodtide?

Early in the contemporary renaissance of the Atlantic salmon fly, people had to delve for information on tying such poetically named flies. The wave of publishing that accompanied the popularity of fly-fishing in the 1970s promoted the most commonly used flies, the Atlantic salmon fly not being among them. During that decade, however, there were a handful of authors and flytyers who were crucial in propagating this budding revival. One of them was Joseph D. Bates, who had published eight books on all types of fishing when *Atlantic Salmon Flies & Fishing* was released in 1970. The book did not take the reader step by step through the tying of the different types of Atlantic salmon patterns, but half of it included dressings for many well-known flies from Europe, the United States, and Canada, along with accounts of their origins. Anyone familiar with basic tying techniques and possessing the essential materials could turn to the dressings in Bates's book and tie a simple feather-wing or hair-wing fly.

Long before the appearance of *Atlantic Salmon Flies & Fishing*, Bates had begun to collect Atlantic salmon flies. To him, the flies were significant as more than tackle. They were a record of important periods and developments in angling history. In his abiding affection for that history, he also collected books, from some of the earliest texts to the most recent, emphasizing

DYED
LADY AMHERST
PHEASANT

fly-fishing but covering all aspects of angling. Bates exhibited selections from his collection, mostly on the east coast, and made the flies available for study to eager tyers in their quest for information. In his research, Bates was an avid correspondent who wrote regularly over many years to a number of flytyers and salmon fly enthusiasts, from Megan Boyd and Alex Simpson in Scotland to Syd Glasso in the Northwest of the United States. Whether by sharing his knowledge and his collection or by inspiring others through his example, he prompted Atlantic salmon fly tyers to study the history of their craft and the achievements of their predecessors. During the last decade of his life, Bates worked on his final book, devoted to the history of the Atlantic salmon fly. By the time *The Art of the Atlantic Salmon Fly* was published in 1987, less than a year before his death, it had a sizable audience of flytyers and collectors that he was partially responsible for creating.

Many tyers had acquired Bates's earlier book for its fly dressings and several color plates, and for its historical anecdotes. But neither it nor its successor explained the specific techniques flytyers needed for dressing Atlantic salmon flies. Enterprising researchers aware of what to look for, and where

to look, sought out the most significant instructional books of the twentieth century, which were those by T. E. Pryce-Tannatt and Eric Taverner. If they were fortunate, they were aware of George Kelson's *The Salmon Fly* of 1895 or Francis Francis's *A Book on Angling* of 1863, or some of the other, rarer nineteenth century texts. Some flytyers experimented with Atlantic salmon flies by tying the examples they found in modern fishing encyclopedias or in such notable books as those by Bill Blades and J. Edson Leonard, which were popular for their trout patterns and instructions.

It was Bill Blades's *Fishing Flies and Fly Tying* that Poul Jorgensen first used when he began to tie flies. Most of all, he was fortunate to have been tutored by Blades himself. If Jorgensen had devoted himself only to flies for trout and salt water, the subject of his first two books, he still would have been among the highly respected angling authors. When he came out in 1978 with his third book, *Salmon Flies*, it ensured

AFRICAN GRAY PARROT

SCARLET IBIS

his place in the history of the Atlantic salmon fly and guaranteed that the popularity of tying salmon flies would continue throughout the 1980s. The color image of the full-dress Durham Ranger on the cover of his pivotal book introduces chapters of instructions and clear step-by-step photographs for tying a broad range of salmon flies, from feather-wings to hair-wings to dry flies. Jorgensen approached the subject from a practical point of view, as someone who fished the flies he tied. He also appreciated their artistry and acknowledged their history. Nearly every tyer in this book you are reading, and many, many who are not, used Jorgensen's book as the foundation on which to build their own work.

Shortly after Jorgensen's book was released, he taught one of his first Atlantic salmon fly classes at Hunter's Angling Supplies in New Boston, New Hampshire. Bill Hunter may not have been surprised that the class filled up the dining room of the house that also served as his shop, but he was struck by the band of "auditors" standing outside the window and eagerly

peering in at the lessons taking place around the dining-room table. Like Jorgensen, Hunter dressed flies for his own fishing. Fond of the traditional patterns, he tied classic feather-wing salmon flies for use on the rivers of Canada. Over the next few years, Hunter's Angling became synonymous with the Atlantic salmon fly as Hunter himself began to teach classes and to stock the materials that other tyers needed for their flies. With few other shops offering salmon fly tying classes, people from around the country made the pilgrimage to the small town of New Boston, and by the early 1980s, Hunter was traveling outside New England to teach classes that people still remember as being instrumental to their tying.

Not all of the flytyers who bought Jorgensen's book or took classes or learned on their own became impassioned with tying such complex flies, but many of those who did began to teach others and to share their knowledge. The flytyers who took up the Atlantic salmon fly in the early 1980s benefited from the other resources that had become available. With the reprinting in the late 1970s of George Kelson's *The Salmon Fly* and of Pryce-Tannatt's *How to Dress Salmon Flies* in a new edition with color plates of flies, people were introduced to two of the most important texts. They also were inspired to discover the multitude of books from the nineteenth and early twentieth centuries containing patterns, dressings, and instructions.

As the ranks of Atlantic salmon fly tyers have expanded,

BLEACHED GOLDEN PHEASANT CREST

RIFLE BIRD

more have entered the field intent on learning how to tie flies as a form of artistic expression rather than to produce flies for their own fishing. A friendly controversy developed, and still exists, about what should, or should not, be the reason for making a salmon fly. One side holds that the only motivation for tying a salmon fly—any fly, in fact—is to deceive a fish, and that the proper salmon fly possesses qualities that enable it to be used effectively on the stream. The other camp, who may or may not fish for salmon, find their rewards by adhering to the format of a traditional fly but make modifications and compromises for the sake of design and artistry, not for function. The views of both sides are valid. What flytyer, on the one hand, would want to spend eight, ten, twelve hours at the vise tying a meticulous feather-wing fly only to lose it on the stream or in a fish, or to have its carefully assembled symmetry rearranged on the first cast? On the other hand, what flytyer would not enjoy reveling in the freedom to conjure up a spellbinding creation on the graceful armature of a hook, aware that it will never be taken to the river but will be framed, indeed enshrined, as an object of contemplation?

The twenty-three Atlantic salmon fly tyers in this book evince many points of view along the spectrum between the functional fly and the exhibition fly. What they all share is a fascination with the challenges and fulfillment of the creative process, of the potential of hands, imagination, and material to make a work that other sets of eyes can appreciate. The object of their intense devotion happens to assume the shape of an Atlantic salmon fly, but it speaks, as all art forms do, of the continuation of a particular tradition, of the unfolding of personal vision, and of the hallmarks of individual style. Like the Atlantic salmon, we need not know what the salmon fly represents, or what it is made of, to be lured by it. We are drawn instinctively to its mystery and its magic.

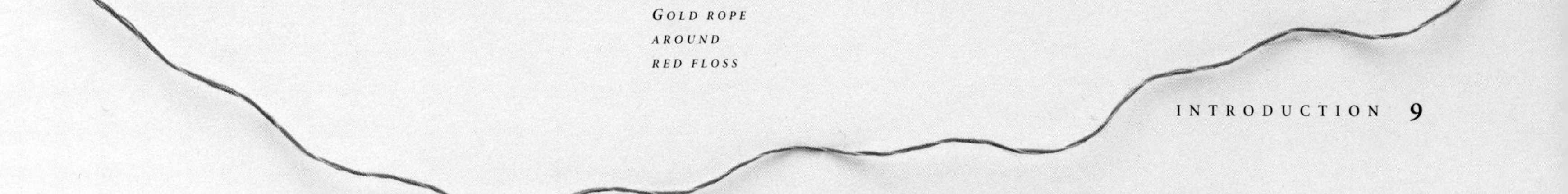

GOLD ROPE
AROUND
RED FLOSS

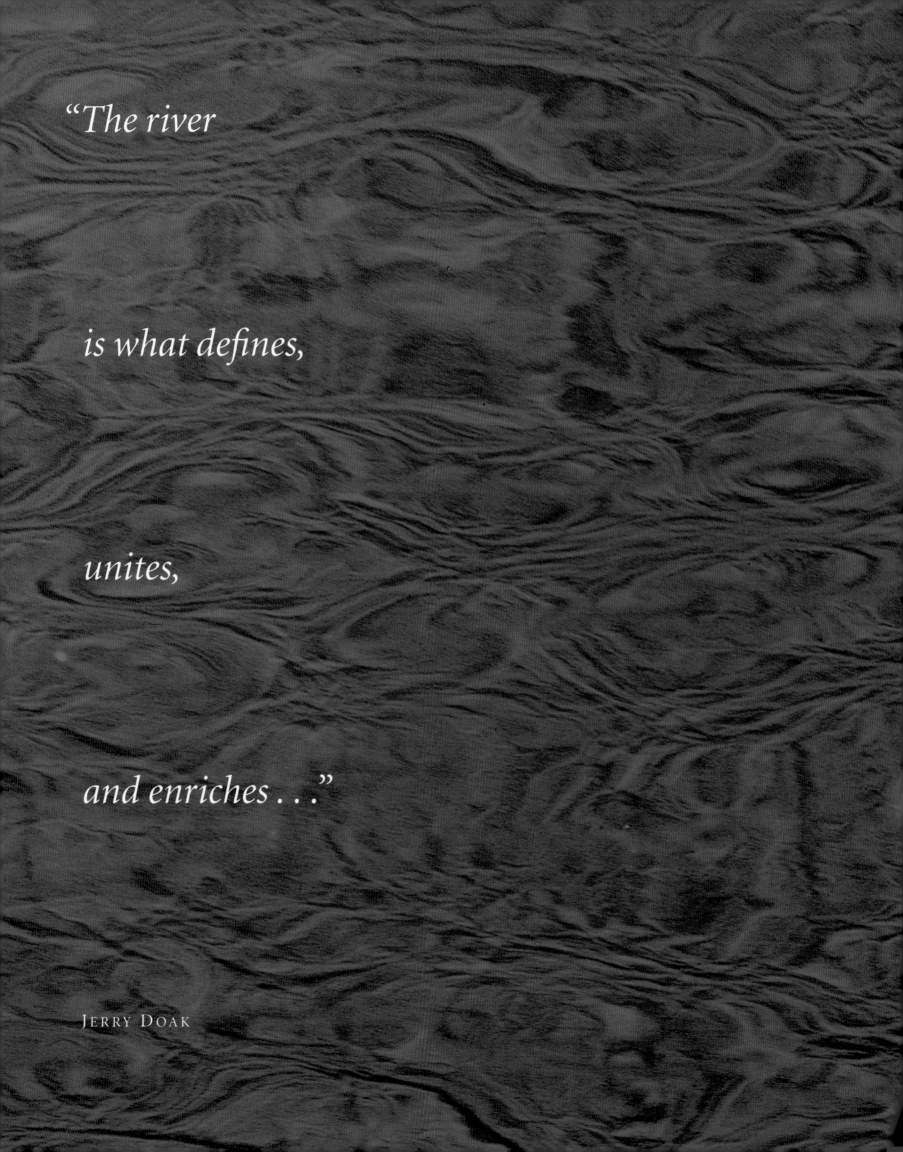

"The river

is what defines,

unites,

and enriches . . ."

Jerry Doak

Canada

Warren Duncan

Buck Bug
Copper Killer
Cosseboom
Green Butt
Green Machine
Hairy Mary
Squirrel Tail
Undertaker

Jerry Doak

Black Dose
Copper Killer
Oriole
Rutledge Fly

WARREN DUNCAN

SAINT JOHN, NEW BRUNSWICK

When I was young, I fished for trout rather than for Atlantic salmon. My family lived in Campbellton, a railroad town on the north shore of New Brunswick at the mouth of the Restigouche River. My father worked for the railroad and had a hunting camp in the woods on a tributary of the Upsalquitch River just for himself and his buddies. The camps in that area could not be reached by car. The best way to get there was to take the train. The old I.N.R., as it was called, used to stop at every hunting camp along the way. We went to the camp in the summer so that my father could get it ready for the hunting season. While he cut wood, my mother and sister and I picked blueberries and strawberries. I fished for brook trout in Grog Brook, a phenomenal stream because it was so remote. Occasionally a grilse would come up the brook. I caught one—on a spinning rod—and I was an excited young fellow.

The people who lived in Campbellton could not afford to fish the Restigouche. Most of the river is private, which made fishing an expensive sport. Even if people wanted to fish the part that isn't private, they needed a very large canoe with a motor, which was also expensive. The few local people who fished a little back then, such as my friend Ralph Billingsley, guided. It was surprising that the locals had no animosity toward the visiting sports. One reason was that salmon fishing boosted the area's whole economy. The millionaires who came to the Restigouche Salmon Club employed so many people, paid good wages, and tipped very well. The reasoning back then was if you couldn't afford to do something, you didn't begrudge it to somebody else.

After I moved to Saint John in 1971, I heard about the Hammond River. I didn't catch anything the first couple of times I fished there. Then, on my first day fishing the Big Hole on the Hammond, I hooked a grilse on a Hammond River Bug and landed it. I think he hooked me better than I hooked him. It was incredible. For the next year or two, I fished salmon heavy, on the Hammond and other local rivers. One spring, I couldn't find a Magog Smelt, a fly I had used the year before with good luck. I stopped into a sporting goods store and bought a flytying kit for five dollars. I tried to imitate what I remembered about the Magog Smelt and tied a number of other flies. A friend loaned me *Art Flick's Master Fly Tying Guide*. I read through it and saw Dave Whitlock's patterns. I never knew there were patterns for flies and started tying the flies in the book.

On a visit to Campbellton, I was proudly telling my father how I could tie flies. He suggested that I visit Ralph Billingsley, who lived across the street. I went to Ralph's. In his basement he had an immaculately clean fly shop, the most packed and compact place you've ever seen. Ralph had tied salmon flies, fished, and guided in the Restigouche area since the 1950s. He showed me what tying flies was all about—because, really, I knew nothing. I went to Campbellton a number of times that winter and on each visit spent two or three days tying salmon flies with Ralph in his basement. Then I went with him to fish the Restigouche, some of the best salmon water in the world: big deep pools, lots of fish. The water is pristine and crystal clear. You can see a dime thirty feet down and tell if it's head or tails. Ralph and I have spent eighteen years fishing the Restigouche,

OPPOSITE, CLOCKWISE
FROM TOP LEFT ROW:

Green Butt
Green Machine
Undertaker
Buck Bug
Hairy Mary
Cosseboom
Copper Killer
Undertaker
Squirrel Tail

the Kedgwick, and the Little Main, and on those early trips I got into some big salmon, twenty, twenty-four, twenty-eight pounders.

Once I learned to tie, I needed to look for materials. Good materials were hard to find in New Brunswick. No one in this part of the country sold materials for salmon flies except for Wally Doak, who was on the Miramichi. I started going to Doaktown to buy materials from him and talk to him about patterns. Then I saw the ad Bill Hunter ran the first year he opened Hunter's Angling Supplies in New Boston, New Hampshire. He sent me the catalog. The materials I wanted were in there, but it was hard to know what they were really like. I sent in an order and received the most beautiful materials I had ever used. When I ordered again, I called Bill because I had some questions. He told me which materials to use for the flies I was tying and sent them to me.

About three years after I started ordering from Bill, we were talking on the telephone and he told me that he had just fished the Restigouche at Brandy Brook camp. I asked him if he had noticed the flies there. "Yes," he said, "beautifully tied flies." "Those are my flies," I told him. "You tied those?" he said. "I should get you to tie for the store." That fall he called me and asked about coming to fish in the area. He called back and asked if he could bring a friend. The friend was Poul Jorgensen. To a beginning flytyer, that was unbelievably exciting. I knew who Poul was and I had his book, *Salmon Flies*, which is the best one ever written on tying Atlantic salmon flies.

After Poul and Bill came to Saint John, Bill invited me to New Boston to take Poul's class on Atlantic salmon flies. The first fly he did was a hair-wing pattern, the Lady Joan. After we tied that, Poul started on a married-wing fly. I had no interest in it because I was looking for flies that I could sell and fish with. All I wanted to do was practice what we had already learned. I went up to Bill's tying room in the attic and tied Lady Joans. Every hour Bill came up to see how I was doing. I was unable to make the collar hackle on the fly flow the way I wanted. Bill came up again after I had been there for about six hours. "What's your problem?" he said. "I can't put a collar hackle on right," I told him. "That's simple." he said. "Use a hen neck." I was using saddle hackle for the collar. I had never heard of a hen neck, the cheapest material in flytying. Bill showed me how to put it on. Zip, zip, zip, and that was it. I couldn't believe it. I sat up there until three in the morning

folding neck hackles and putting them on hooks. It was the single greatest improvement in my tying. When I started to tie for Bill, I sent him five hundred various flies. Bill did not accept flies that were less than perfect, and he returned the ones he didn't like. We sent them back and forth until he was satisfied with them, which improved my tying immensely.

After fishing the Restigouche for so many years, I knew I had to go to the Miramichi River. When I started fishing the Miramichi in the late 1970s, I was a Restigouche flytyer. For the fast-running water of the Restigouche, you wanted a big fly tied on a double hook. I was trying to adapt Restigouche flies for the Miramichi, which just didn't work. Nobody wanted to fish on the Miramichi with the heavily dressed salmon flies. The popular Miramichi patterns were very simple ones that could be tied small and on single hooks. As I fished the Miramichi more, talked to other anglers, and looked into their fly boxes, I began to change my style of tying. The greatest difference between Restigouche and Miramichi flies is size rather than dressing. For years, flies in sizes 2, 4, and 6 were standard on the Restigouche, sometimes as large as 5/0. The materials used in these flies do not lend themselves to smaller flies. Finding gray fox for a thousand size 10 Rats, for instance, would be prohibitive. Also, the palmered body hackle on many Restigouche flies is out of place on very small flies.

The flytying traditions on the Restigouche and the Miramichi developed very separately. The only two tyers in the province who ever received any publicity were J. C. Arseneault in Atholville and Wally Doak in Doaktown. They were also the two tyers in the province who built up their businesses from nothing. Their styles and the type of flies they tied were totally different. In the 1940s and 1950s, local people did very little traveling. I remember as a kid traveling six and one-half hours from Campbellton down to Newcastle to visit a friend's grandmother. Now it would take me an hour and forty-five minutes. Back then, it would have been another three hours to Doaktown. So if Wally Doak wanted to go see Clovie Arseneault, it was an eight-hour trip by car. There wasn't the exchange of information that there is now.

Restigouche flies were Clovie Arseneault's forte, though he tied flies for people all over the world. Clovie had boxes of salmon flies at all the camps along the river. In the fall, after the season closed, he picked up the boxes, and during the winter, he filled them with flies for the following spring. The people from the camps picked up their boxes full of flies, and each box had a bill on it. When Arseneault was first tying in the 1920s, no one else in New Brunswick, not even Wally Doak, was making a living tying flies. Clovie was in business longer than anyone in this part of the country, but he seldom received the credit he deserved for being a pioneer because his demeanor was very gruff and he was so hard to get along with.

When you first went into his store in Atholville, Clovie didn't speak to you. He sat with his back to the counter. You could stand there for ten or fifteen minutes before he turned around. When he did, you had better know what you wanted because he was going to stop tying flies. I was afraid it was going to cost me my life to interrupt him. When I had just started tying flies and was going to the Restigouche, I thought I'd go see what Clovie had in his store. When he turned on me—and he turned so suddenly—he barked, "What do you want?" I couldn't think of what I wanted. I said, "I want to see some flies, Mr. Arseneault." "Of course you want to see some flies," he yelled back. "What you think we are doing here?" I was so terrified that the only fly I could think of was a Mickey Finn. He started pulling out drawers and slamming the flies on the counter. I asked for three flies. I gave him three dollars and ran out of the store. That was the front he put on so that talkers wouldn't waste his time.

Clovie was the same way the day Joseph Bates walked in when he was working on *Atlantic Salmon Flies & Fishing.* As the story goes, Joe offered to include some of Clovie's flies in his book and thereby popularize his business. Without turning around from the tying bench, Clovie merely quoted him the price per fly and asked how many he wanted. Of course, Clovie sold every fly he tied and felt he didn't need anyone proposing to give him recognition. When Bates asked for flies for the book, Clovie told him the price, period. At which time Bates walked out of the store and never gave Clovie credit for anything. It's a crime, since Bates was one of the people who could have recorded what Clovie did.

Bates's book is valuable in so many ways, especially for the patterns and their histories, and I use it frequently in my own tying. But he overlooked Clovie and never recognized him for tying many of the Rat series of flies, which are usually attributed to Roy Angus Thomson. An article in the winter 1965 *Atlantic Salmon Journal* discusses Clovie's invention of some of the Rats and of the Rusty Rat in particular, one of the

best producers on the Restigouche that season. In the 1940s, Joseph Pulitzer was fishing at Brandy Brook on the Restigouche with one of Clovie's large Black Rats or, according to other stories, with a Rat. After Pulitzer took two salmon on the fly, the peacock on the body started to unwind and revealed the dark orange floss Clovie had used to build up the body of the fly. Pulitzer caught so many fish with the fly, including a forty-one pounder, that he asked Clovie to tie a similar fly, which was the Rusty Rat.

After Clovie died in 1980, people tried to characterize his flies. There was little consistency to his tying, unless he was tying an order for the same camp. It was impossible to separate his flies into early flies and later flies. He just sat there and tied, using what was on the desk. On one Rusty Rat he might use saddle hackle, on another hen neck, and on a third dry fly hackle. There often was no reason for the choice other than that's the material he happened to have in quantity and that's what he used. And nobody criticized him. There were so many salmon in the river and so few people fishing that the specific material didn't make a crucial difference. I even had flies where local tyers had tied little pieces of rock on the bottom of the bodies for extra weight. The rock was tied on with coarse thread, then the rest of the fly was tied over the top of it.

People look at Arseneault's flies and think they are rough. He was tying on 3/0 and 5/0 hooks, with materials that were around since 1910 and 1920, and with thread that must have been 2/0 or 1/0. The fine threads being pioneered in the United States at the time were scorned by salmon fly tyers as being cobwebs, and were not considered strong enough for the large flies and the beating they took from eighteen-foot rods and fast water. That approach characterized Clovie's tying. He didn't try to be esthetic. He knew what would catch fish and what his customers wanted.

A few people tried to get into the business in the Restigouche area, but nobody was going to take a chance on buying someone else's flies when Clovie had tied successful Restigouche flies for decades. The only other tyer in the Restigouche area anyone knew about was Joe Duguay from Dalhousie, who started tying thirty years after Clovie did. He had a little shop in his house and in the summer parked his trailer on the banks of the Restigouche. He tied flies and sold them out of the trailer. He was in competition with Clovie, but he was nowhere as good a tyer as Clovie was. He invented a lot of oddball patterns and he sold a lot of flies. After Clovie died, Ralph Billingsley inherited most of Clovie's business from the camps, because no one was interested in continuing the business. Ralph is known for the same kind of Restigouche fly—a very large fly but very beautifully tied. He supplies most of the clubs on the Restigouche, and during the winter he probably ties seven or eight thousand salmon flies.

Most of all, the Atlantic salmon flies for the New Brunswick rivers had to have durability. That is still the key. Like Clovie, I tie durable flies, and I'm not trying to tie a perfect fly to be photographed. That's flytying in New Brunswick. That's how Clovie Arseneault tied flies. That's how Wally Doak tied flies. And I certainly emulate their type of tying and their type of business. I make refinements which are possible by using modern tinsels and threads. The current school of flytying advocates using a minimum number of turns to tie on each part of a fly so that it doesn't have any bulk. The problem is that you can pull the tail right out of the fly. Before I even tie the body, I have put a hundred or so turns of thread on the hook. As a result I get a very durable fly. That's the reputation I want for my tying and for my shop in Saint John.

Poul Jorgensen titled his book *Salmon Flies: Their Character, Style, and Dressing.* I know tyers who swear that flies don't have character but, to me, character is what allows a salmon angler to look in a fly box at fifty flies—all tied exactly the same—and pick out the one that is going to take a fish. I can do that with my own flies. It might be hard to see the differences. Maybe the body has a certain taper or is a little thicker. Something in one of those flies makes me want to fish it. I call it character. A flytyer who does not fish cannot put character in a fly. A fisherman can recognize character and put it in his flies. This is not to say that only fishermen can tie flies. However, anyone who ties flies without input from fishermen is very seldom successful. Megan Boyd is a case in point. As she developed her tying style, it is evident that she spoke to hundreds of fishermen, and her flies are among the best examples available today of the flytyer's ability to put character in a salmon fly.

Anybody can develop a fly pattern. Standards have been around for a long time and they are hard to improve, but I thought if I ever invented a fly, I would call it the Undertaker. I came up with the Undertaker in 1979. My friend Chris Russell was fishing the Nashwaak, without success. He saw a chap upriver who landed a fish and lost it, then landed another fish.

As the man fished, he broke off the point of the hook on a back cast. Chris saw him change flies, drop the damaged fly, then continue fishing. When the man left, Chris picked up the fly and brought it home. We couldn't find anything like it in the flytying books, so I started playing with the pattern. I didn't like the black wool in the body and substituted peacock herl. I used gold for the rib because the Rats use gold and I love the Rat series of flies. I tied up three or four Undertakers in size 2 and 4 doubles. The first time I used it, on the Hammond River, I caught a twenty-four-pound salmon. Then Chris used it on the Kedgwick and got a thirty-eight-pound salmon. Bill Hunter put it in his catalog. The next year, it was in the Orvis catalog, then in L. L. Bean's. All of a sudden the Undertaker was a fly.

The Undertaker is essentially another black fly with a double butt. Black flies are standard on many Atlantic salmon rivers, and there are many variations, depending on the river. The Miramichi was always considered a black river, hence the Black Bear Green Butt, Shady Lady, and Undertaker style of fly. It didn't matter what fly you used as long as it was black. Green and yellow are also considered very good Miramichi colors. The Restigouche is another good green and yellow river. The St. Jean in Québec is a black and white river because such patterns as the Skunk, Molson, and Lady Amherst do well there. There's no explanation for it, and no sense to it, but somehow certain flies in certain colors became associated with certain rivers.

With salmon fishing, there are no guarantees that you will catch a fish, and nobody can tell you before you go out what's going to happen. There are more theories on why salmon do or don't take a fly. The river is low and the water is warm. The moon is in the wrong phase. The color of the canoe is wrong. Some guy downriver is running a motor. He might be three miles away but he is scaring the fish. This guy is using a fly that is too big. That guy is using a fly that is too small. This guy is wading too far out in the river. That guy is not wading out far enough. All these excuses. Someone says that you can't use a fluorescent green line. Then a twelve-year-old throws a pile of green line in the river, and when the current finally straightens it out, he's got a twelve-pound salmon. I've gone on fishing trips where I haven't caught fish, where I've wrecked brand-new trucks, where I've broken rods. But I've never had a bad fishing trip in my life. Fishing becomes secondary. It's the trip that's important.

JERRY DOAK

Realizing that I wanted to be involved in fly-fishing as a career was a gradual discovery. My father Wallace never pressured me to carry on the business he started in 1946. If anything, he would say, "Are you sure you want to get mixed up in all this?" But in the back of my mind, I knew that the opportunity was open if I wanted to develop it. Dad grew up in Doaktown and had an intense love for the area. The older I got and the broader my perspective became through my travels and my education, the more I began to see that there was a magnetism about the business and about the Miramichi River.

As a child, I was persistent enough that Dad started to give me odd jobs in the store. He had built the store in the front yard of the house where I was born. He spent a lot of time there and worked hard, so he liked to go fishing by himself one afternoon a week. He preferred trout fishing over salmon fishing because fishing for trout tends to be a more solitary pursuit. I remember the first day I ran the store alone. I was about twelve years old. I took in what was a fair amount of money in those days and was proud of myself. Dad was not the sort to tell me how he felt, but when he came home, I could tell he was pleased. I got a glimpse of the thrill of doing business, and an appreciation of the approval implicit in each customer's purchase. The experience of taking care of the store that day stuck with me through my teenage years.

LEFT: *Black Dose*

I also had to be persistent in order to convince Dad to teach me flytying. He was easily irritated by distractions, and I used to sit too close and breathe over his shoulder, doing annoying things like chewing gum and swallowing loudly. I watched as much as I could get away with and managed to pick up some of his techniques. Everything he did was a secret.

That was a common attitude among flytyers of his day because information was passed on by word of mouth rather than learned from books. He would say, "Don't ever tell anyone how I evened this hair," or "Don't show anyone how I folded this hackle." When Charlie DeFeo came to the area to fish, he would visit the store, and for some reason Dad felt morally bound not to divulge any of the tying techniques that Charlie shared with him.

The first fly I tied was a Green Butt Bear Hair, which Dad called a Conrad, after Charles Conrad, who popularized it in the mid-1950s. It was a very primitive effort. The first comment Dad made was, "You forgot the tail on the fly"—not "The body looks good." Dad was such a fast learner that he didn't always understand the work other people might need to tie flies. I remember liking the Cosseboom better than the Green Butt Bear Hair, but Dad felt I should begin by tying the fly with the least expensive materials, which was practical because I went through a lot of flies. I tied several hundred flies before he deemed them good enough to sell. He was remarkably more tolerant of my flies than I thought he might have been. I probably tied several thousand flies before I felt they were at all satisfactory.

When I started tying more regularly for the store, I produced what was most in demand, which was a variety of standard hair-wing patterns, such as Green Butt Bear Hairs, Red Butt Squirrel Tails, and Cossebooms. Not until I took over the business did I start to tie Rusty Rats, Silver Rats, Orange Blossoms, and more diverse Atlantic salmon patterns. When Dad ran the business, he considered what might be the most pragmatic fly for me to tie. What materials are readily available? Where is the demand? The demand was much different in the 1960s than it is now. Then, it was narrowly defined as the salmon flies used on the Miramichi. Now, the shop's demand is defined by whether a customer is going to Iceland, Norway, or Labrador for Atlantic salmon, or is fishing Bombers for steelhead on the west coast.

I am not sure what originally attracted me to flytying. Obviously I realized tying offered the potential to make extra income, although I knew I would never earn a huge amount of money. But there was so much more than that. Learning to tie flies was a way to be close to my father by doing the same thing he was doing. The more time I spent with Dad in the store, the more I understood the nature of his approach to the business and to flytying. Dad was a committed Christian, and this instilled within him a deep sense of personal and professional integrity. He had a very strong concept of fair treatment for all customers, regardless of their station in life or the amount of money in their pockets. "When a customer comes in the door," he used to say, "it doesn't matter who they are. They are all fishermen." I always thought that, if I were on the other side of the counter, I would want to be treated that way. I try to do that today.

Dad also had definite ideas about flytying. He never tried to be a fly inventor, in keeping with his belief that there were enough fly patterns on the market and there was more demand than he could supply. Dad was not plagued by the boredom that frequently leads some tyers to be more rambling in their tying habits and techniques. He felt it was imperative for a commercial tyer's flies to have a consistency in patterning and in the quality of the tying. Many tyers tend to be adventurous, one week tying a dozen flies of a particular pattern, then the next week changing materials, color, or style to suit their mood. Customers need to know that, when they come back year after year, they can find the same pattern tied the same way. Tying flies for Dad's store gave me a taste for the repetitive, or at least a tolerance of it. It is one of the things for which

commercial tyers don't adequately prepare themselves, and one of the things I have tried to pass on to the tyers who work in the store now. When a tyer sits down to tie three or four hundred Undertakers, it can sometimes be difficult to find the next one exciting.

Dad did have his own interpretations of flies, like the Cosseboom. He tied it with a darker body than the original, and with a black head rather than a red head. At the shop we offer both the traditional Cosseboom and what we call the Miramichi Cosseboom, which is Dad's version and has been popular on the river for a long time. Unless we intentionally do a variation of a fly, which is rare, or unless a material becomes unavailable, we make every possible effort to offer in the store the same flies Dad sold, even though other tyers may have a different interpretation of a particular pattern. Certain flies are more productive on the Miramichi than they are on other rivers, more by virtue of the intensity of their use than because of the susceptibility of the salmon or the effectiveness of the patterns. When a customer trusts me to recommend flies I have found to be proven successes, the patterns invariably fall within that list of old favorites which seem preferred by nearly all Miramichi fishermen.

Amateur flytyers have the luxury of being inventive, and I must confess that I am as guilty as the next tyer of being a little adventurous for my own purposes. I fall prey to curiosity and tie a pattern that is a little different, using the knowledge I have supposedly gained over the years. I go fishing with the thought, "Now I've really stumbled on the right fly. This is going to work the best." Usually the salmon say, "Big deal. I want a Green Machine." The salmon are in a prespawning condition when they come up the river, and they are not feeding, which makes them very unpredictable. The bottom line is that the salmon have a great way of deflating egos. People who

ABOVE, CLOCKWISE
FROM TOP:

Oriole
Rutledge Fly
Copper Killer

are otherwise successful in all their pursuits, including fly-fishing and flytying, can come here and strike out along with the rest. So when Dad said it doesn't matter who a fisherman is, that is very much the salmon's perspective. It is hard to figure them out. That's why they are so thrilling and challenging.

If I were going to tie a fly simply for the esthetic satisfaction, it would be a fully dressed Atlantic salmon fly, mainly because of the beauty and complexity. Dad taught me the basics of tying standard feather-wings like the Blue Charm, but he felt that feather-wings were not used much anymore and I didn't need to know how to tie them. So I had to learn feather-wings on my own. I started tying the more complex patterns in the early 1980s, and although I love to tie them, time constraints usually don't permit it. When people say they want my flies to frame, I usually feel a little apprehensive. Like my father, I have never been preoccupied with being singled out for my flies. Although I take my vocation seriously inasmuch as it impacts the store's reputation, I have never sought recognition as a flytyer. My only accomplishment is that I am my father's son, and I tend to defer to his work and his reputation.

I look back on Dad's era as the time when the foundation was laid for the traditions and industry that we have now. Dad was born in 1912 and lived through some very formative decades. In the 1930s and 1940s, the demand for flies increased as outfitting started to get off the ground. In the 1950s, people started to fish more enthusiastically, more sportingly, with flies. So if I were to tie a fly representative of the area, it would be a fly evocative of that transitional era on the Miramichi. It would be, for instance, an Oriole with a simple dyed mallard wing, more understated and less ornate than a full-dress pattern. The tyers who developed salmon flies in North America worked from a reductionist point of view and were very utilitarian in their approach. In recent years, flies have become very buggy and flamboyant, overhackled and overdressed. The ideal fly for me goes back to the days when patterns had a discreet form and a certain consistency, when a good flytyer was recognized not for how many expensive hackles he could fit on a bug but for how neatly he laid the feathers into place or finished a head.

Ira Gruber, who fished the Miramichi from the 1940s through the 1960s, was part of that developmental era. Gruber hired Everett Price to teach him how to tie flies. I was very young when Gruber still fished in the area, but I remember Dad mentioning him frequently. His salmon flies became popular by virtue of the considerable amount of time he spent fishing them. Flies like the Oriole and Reliable were very neat and compact, the silhouettes very distinct and linear. There was nothing haphazard about them.

Burt Miner, another tyer from that era, is someone I remember well. He tied all the Copper Killers for Dad's store. I would go up to Burt's little house in Doaktown and watch him tie. He was a heavy smoker who rolled his own cigarettes. There was so much smoke in the room that I could barely see the fly in the vise. He would roll a cigarette with one hand and tie a Copper Killer with the other. He was a very colorful character, a legendary figure. He exuded the river, and was one of many people for whom the river was like their bloodstream. It was the way they derived their living in the summer, and it was what they looked forward to all winter. I have always associated Burt with the Copper Killer. It is a great fly on the Cains River, and Burt was an avid Cains River guide. I have never had a passion to discover the actual origin of the fly. It's almost as if the legend is more interesting than the facts would be. Traditions like that almost transcend the factual and aspire to the mystical. Anytime you look back on history, you are bound to have your own image of it. The facts can sometimes rob you of your vision.

J. C. Arseneault was still alive when I took over Dad's shop. In the fall of 1977, I decided to go to meet him in his shop in Atholville. Arseneault was a larger-than-life figure. His little shop on the Restigouche River flourished for many years under his knowledgeable and sometimes abrasive direction. I knew that he and Dad had a mutual respect, though they weren't close friends. Yet Dad had the impression that Arseneault did not think too highly of the Miramichi. The Restigouche was always associated with a more affluent fisherman than was the Miramichi. In spite of this, Dad always spoke of Arseneault in very positive terms. When I went into Arseneault's shop, I did not identify myself immediately. I just struck up a conversation. We had an enjoyable talk, and in the course of it I told him who I was and what I was doing. He was very cordial. "Oh yes," he said, "I've known of your father for years and I hear so much about him." Arseneault pulled open a drawer filled with flies and said, "Do you know what these are?" I identified this fly and that fly. "You're pretty sharp," he said. "You've been at this for a while." It was if he was testing me—and I passed.

A year before that, my father retired because he found out he had cancer. My brother George and I ran the shop for the first year and enjoyed it immensely. George, who is ten years older than me, was a high school teacher in Fredericton. Since it was not really practical for him to move permanently back to Doaktown, he opened a smaller version of the Doaktown store in Fredericton in 1978. I was on my own. The fishing was good in 1977, but in 1978 it was a disaster. In 1979, the year my father died, it was not great, and in 1980 the commercial fishery was restored in Miramichi Bay after an eight-year moratorium. In 1981 and 1982, the fishing suffered, and in 1983, it flattened completely.

The first week in June of 1983 was good. There was a considerable amount of water and many salmon came in. In mid-June, the commercial nets went in, and after that, virtually no fish came up the river. Pool after pool that should have held hundreds of salmon had nothing. There was a great deal of anger up and down the river, which resulted in the formation of a committee to spearhead the effort to solve the problem. We organized meetings and were able to find significant information on the economic value of the sports fishery as opposed to the commercial fishery. We drew up a position paper and lobbied the government. The effort was successful, and the commercial fishery was eliminated in 1984. There was a huge and immediate difference. In 1985, the fishing was better, and in 1986, we had a bumper year. Now one hundred fifty thousand salmon and grilse come up the Miramichi each season.

Seeing the Miramichi River rebound was a thrill. If the river had not recovered, I would be a much poorer person, whether I were in this business or completely dissociated from it. The river is what defines, unites, and enriches the lives of all of us as native Miramichiers. The survival instinct of the Atlantic salmon is a striking testimony to the intricacy of God's creation. The fish are threatened by a huge number of predators when they leave the Miramichi. They go thousands of miles out to sea and come back to spawn within feet of where they were born. In the fall I have stood with my kids and watched salmon jumping over falls or fighting over rocks trying to return to their native spawning beds. They fight hard, they struggle up the river, they spawn and make more fish, and they return to the sea. It is an expression of the raw magnificence of nature. Who you are or where you come from pales in comparison to the mysteries of the Miramichi. The river equalizes everybody, and it is as if the salmon have been put there to reinforce that.

"You can say

what you like

but everyone

is puzzled over

why a salmon

takes a fly."

MEGAN BOYD

Europe and Japan

MEGAN BOYD

Blue Doctor

Brora

Childers

Torrish

HANS DE GROOT

The Macallan

Royal Lochnagar

STEWART CANHAM

Dusty Miller

JIMMY YOUNGER

Arndilly Fancy

Black Doctor

Dusty Miller

Garry Dog

Munro Killer

Watson's Fancy

KEN SAWADA

Daybreak

Un-Married Angel

MEGAN BOYD

When I started to tie salmon flies, all the flies made then were the feather-wings fishermen were using on the Helmsdale and Brora rivers in the north of Scotland. Those early flies were on gut-eye hooks and they were all the difficult ones—Jock Scotts, Black Doctors, Pophams, Childerses. My father used to fish occasionally, and he would come home with a fly or two he found on the riverbanks. They were lovely to look at. I said, "I'd like to make them"—and that's what set me going. Flytyers were few and far between then, and I thought tying would be a good job to do.

My father did not tie flies. He worked as a water bailiff on the Brora River after our family came to Brora. On the Countess of Sutherland's side of the river there was a keeper, Bob Trussler, who tied flies. I don't know where he learned—perhaps he just copied patterns he saw on the river. When I was twelve, I started to go to his place to learn to tie. Trussler made a nice fly. He was very good with his hands. Everything that man did was perfection. He made his own furniture for his house and his own sidecar for his motorbike.

To teach me, Bob Trussler put an old, used fly in front of me. We took all the bits and pieces off the hook, then I had to put them back on a smaller hook, a little at a time, as I remembered they should be on the fly. He watched over me as I tied and told me how to make the knots and keep the fly neat, and looked to see if I missed a part. I had to get the body right first, then he showed me how to mix and build the wings. For a number of years I went back and forth to see Bob Trussler. The heads on the flies might be too big—and I wanted to be sure to get them right. I didn't have the money to buy a lot of stock, so I practiced with old flies by cutting them up and putting the parts on smaller hooks. My father found the flies on the stream or the ghillies gave him flies with broken hooks. Gradually I bought materials. Bob Trussler was very good at giving me bits and pieces if someone wanted a fly.

When I left school I was fifteen, and the first order I got was from Sir Charles Clauson, converting a box of gut-eye flies to hooks with metal eyes. I had to take all the materials off the gut-eye hooks and put them on the metal-eye hooks. I cut the materials carefully off each hook, laid them all out, and tied them back on a new hook. It took me twice as long as I thought it would. Somebody later said to me, "What did you charge?" I said, "A lot less than a new fly." "You silly," he said, "you'll never make ends meet that way. You've taken twice as long to do it." "Yes, I know," I said, "but I didn't think I could charge twice as much for them." I suppose I did tie them rather cheaply. I didn't mind. I just liked tying a salmon fly. As long as I was pleased with the finished article and liked looking at it myself, that's all that mattered. I had no interest in fishing, but I never got tired of tying salmon flies.

The Tyser family owned the estate on the north side of the Brora River, and when Jessie Tyser saw that I was doing a decent job, she started to buy all her flies from me. She did not order them one at a time, but a dozen of this and a dozen of that. She had the most beautiful boxes made at Hardy in London especially for the flies. One day Mrs. Tyser wanted a family fly. I had her hair, the children's hair, the parrot's feather, the dog's hair—I put everything into the fly.

In 1935, when I was almost twenty, I moved to the bungalow at Kintradwell, north of Brora, and I lived there for fifty-three years. From the house I had a big view of the coast. There was a long, long lobby with a nice large window at the end. You could stand at the back of the house, look at the North Sea, and think that you were on a boat. The house was built in 1906. Much of it was made from secondhand materials that came off

RIGHT: *Brora*

the shore where there used to be a lot of fishing huts. It was built of corrugated iron, wood, brick, and stone, and was beautifully done by people working with next to nothing in the tool line. There were even carved bits of wood around the fireplace.

I made a big garden seat for myself at the front of the house. I used to sit there and eat all my meals, and not a soul was around. I worked in the house first, then moved to the hut next door and had a big glass window put in. When I sat at my tying bench in the hut next door, I faced the sea and the sun, and I enjoyed it. I could see the main road and in the distance the railway and the golf course.

Fishermen came from all over to fish the Brora and the Helmsdale. They would go home and say, "You can get your flies from Megan Boyd." One fisherman told another, and my business grew and grew. The fishermen usually sent to Hardy in London for all their flies, so they were quite pleased to be able to get them at the riverside. I tied some flies for shops, for Gray and Company and occasionally a special dozen for MacPherson's in Inverness. Then I started to get postal orders from all over, and I couldn't continue supplying the shops because I was so busy. Bob Trussler always said to me, "Never advertise your work. Let your work advertise you." I never put an advert in the paper, or anywhere, in my life.

LEFT: *Childers*

Back then, we tried to tie salmon flies as we saw them in the books. The book I always stuck to was Pryce-Tannatt's *How to Dress Salmon Flies*. It was given to me by a man in Brora, Lacy Sergeantson, who used to tie his own flies. The flies in the book are beautiful and the dressings are very clear. One day a woman came to see me because she wanted to learn to tie flies. I said, "There's one book you want to get. It's Pryce-Tannatt's book. It was given to me by a gentleman in Brora who tied his own flies, a Mr. Sergeantson." "Oh," she said, "That was my father." "Well," I said, "why on earth didn't you learn from your father?" "He wanted to teach me," she said, "but I wouldn't learn." That's always the way. His daughter was seventy-six when she came to me to tie flies. It's just something that you do if you want to. You can't be pushed into it as a job.

Professor Cappell in Glasgow gave me an original George Kelson book from 1895. He always came fishing on the Helmsdale. He wanted me to tie a certain pattern and said, "You'll get it in Kelson's *The Salmon Fly*." I didn't have it so he brought it to me. I used the Kelson book because it had lots

of patterns that weren't in Pryce-Tannatt. When I received the British Empire Medal in 1971, Professor Cappell said, "Do you still have my book?" "Yes," I said, "I find it very useful." "Well," he said, "I think you deserve it. I'm giving it to you."

Many years ago, the hair-wing flies started to become popular. A man in Inverness, Watson, had a shop and came up to the Helmsdale. He made a wee fly called the Hairy Mary. That was one of the first hair-wing flies. It was really the body of a Blue Charm with a wee bunch of hair on top. The Hairy Mary was cheap and easy to make. They were in Watson's shop by the dozens. Everyone was fishing with Hairy Marys and of course they were bound to catch fish. Before I left Kintradwell, quite a few fishermen still came to me and asked for feather-wing flies, and I never refused them. Few tyers now will make a feather-wing for a man going fishing. A bunch of hair will do it, and that's it.

But you can't tie flies in five minutes. It's a job to learn. The man who was running a flytying factory in Helmsdale, north of Brora, came to me and said, "How long does it take to learn to tie salmon flies?" "Oh, heavens," I said, "You need at least five years to learn." "What nonsense," he said, "I saw people tying flies on television, and they do them in five minutes." I said, "Not what I do." He didn't know the difference between trout and salmon flies on the television. It's a job like anything else that you have to learn properly. It took me a quarter of an hour to tie a simple Hairy Mary. People said to me, "Your flies don't come to pieces like the ones in the shop. In two or three casts the tail comes off." I was taught to knot every part as I put it on the fly.

Charles Ackroyd also came to the Brora and Helmsdale to fish. My father knew Charles Ackroyd. By the time I knew him, he was an old man. He built a big house in Brora that is now the Marine Hotel. He was a fine tyer of trout and salmon flies. He had a big black leather book he made himself. Inside were all the feathers he needed to tie a trout fly by the river. He later gave the book to my father. I made quite a few of the Ackroyd salmon flies. Charlie called it the Poor Man's Jock Scott because it was half yellow and half black and had a cinnamon turkey wing, with the jungle cock tied down below. It was quite a nice fly, very simple, and was just as good as a Jock Scott with all of its feathers. Long after Charlie was dead, I made a huge Ackroyd fly for the hotel but it later disappeared.

Quite a few fishermen used the Ackroyd. It was just as

good as any fly. With a fly, you are just lucky that the fish are taking it at the time. You can say what you like but everyone is puzzled over why a salmon takes a fly, because they take all sorts of things. A man once took the gold foil top off his bottle of whisky. He crumpled it and threw it in the water. A salmon came up and grabbed it. Then the man wanted a fly tied the same color. There are endless fishing patterns, and people go on changing them.

A man came to see me with his black labrador. He said, "What about making me a fly?" So I did a simple fly. I made a Hairy Mary body and for a wing put on some black hair from his dog. He was quite happy with the fly. Another

man was sitting in the car waiting for him. He had the most enormous eyebrows you ever saw. He started plucking out hairs from his eyebrows and said, "There you are, Megan, you can put these on a fly for me. If we get a fish, you'll get a bit." When I came home that Sunday night, on the seat at the door was a parcel. It said, "Caught by the Hairy Dog." I knew which fly caught the fish—the one with the black dog hairs. The other man's eyebrows were gray and black. So it was just that the one man was lucky. That's the way I look at it. I always say, "I catch the fishermen and not the fish." People are just

attracted by all the different patterns because they are so lovely to look at.

There's no one more silly than a fisherman. Fishermen try this, they try that. A man has a big fly box and spends all day changing patterns to catch fish. There will be one person who always has his fly in the water and catches far more fish while the other fellows are changing flies. I always say that the fly in the water is the one that catches the fish.

I didn't invent many flies for fishing. John Ropner was the fishing partner of the Countess of Seafield. Between the two of us, we made the Countess of Seafield fly for the Dee River, where the Countess fished. I invented another fly as a brooch, not as a fishing fly. I saw a film where a woman wore a beautiful dress. I thought the colors would be pretty in a salmon fly, and I called it the Opera. I did other brooches and named them after the mountains down on Speyside. The flies were quite attractive to look at, but the fishermen kept me so busy with orders that I had no time to invent flies.

There is one wee fly, a tube fly, that is called the Megan. I didn't invent it. A man who came to me for flies didn't like fishing with tubes. I said, "If you don't like fishing with tubes, why can't you have a fly on a double hook tied the same way as a tube?" So I made this little black and blue fly by putting the hair all around the hook. It must have been fished everywhere. I was told it was the most popular fly in Iceland and it was called the Megan, but it's not my fly. It was just a different way of doing something. A lot of flies are tied that way.

I had masses and masses of letters from people who wanted to buy flies to frame. As long as I was tying flies for the fisherman—which I started off doing to earn my daily bread—I kept doing it. All the other orders had to go to the bottom of the pile. I could have tied two flies a week for framing and charged a high price for them. But all my life I earned my daily bread from the fisherman, and I wasn't going to tell him to go away and that I was doing something else to make money.

I showed tying to a lot of people but I couldn't teach them if they didn't come often enough so I could see how they were getting on. People came from all over to see me tie flies. I showed them what to do. There was only one man I taught who made a decent sort of job. He was Ian Sutherland. When I was helping him, he was a keeper at Gordonbush lodge on the Brora River. Then he went north to Kildonan where he sold his flies to people who fished on the Helmsdale.

Joseph Bates and his wife Helen came to see me once. I remember that because he is the first name in my visitor's book. My sister April said before Joe came, "Why on earth don't you have a visitor's book?" It had never entered my head. So I started a book in 1973, and Joe Bates and his wife Helen were the first to sign it, on May 24. I had all these wonderful people come to see me, people from as far away as Australia and China, and many lords and ladies.

My father was terribly fond of what we call the toffs. I treat everybody as ordinary working people or ordinary everyday people. No one has the right to be different from any other. I never made a fuss, but my father would call them "Sirs" and "Lords." They never got a "Sir" or "Lord" from me, not even Prince Charles. He said, "Hello, Megan, it's nice to see you." I said, "Hello, it's nice of you to have me." And that's all that was said. I didn't call him Prince Charles or anything else, and you weren't expected to. I always thought that was why I was asked here, there, and everywhere—because I was just as I was. I was not put on for everyone. There's no use aping to be different.

Prince Charles wrote me a nice letter when I had to leave Kintradwell. I knew that my eyesight was going because I was making bigger heads on the flies, and once you start to do that, it's no use. My dog was ill at the same time. I was told there was nothing could be done about my eyes. I moved to Brora on August 12, 1988. I remember it because that was the day grouse shooting began, and it's a big day for people traveling north to go hunting. I had hoped to die up in Kintradwell tying flies in my hut. You just don't know that what you planned to do doesn't come out. I just had to make the best of where I was. That's all I could do, but I was always lucky to be doing something that I liked doing.

HANS DE GROOT

ZWANENBURG, HOLLAND

The first time I saw Atlantic salmon flies was when I went to Ireland in 1972 on a holiday. A friend and I fished Lough Currane in County Kerry for sea trout. On these large lakes, one fishes mainly from a boat on the drift. We had stopped at one of the islands in the lake and were having lunch when another boat landed, also for lunch. Inevitably we all started talking about the fishing, and one of the fishermen from the other boat opened his fly box to show me the flies he was using. They were full-dressed salmon flies and looked so beautiful that I immediately knew I wanted to learn how to tie them. Being involved in the graphic arts, I responded to the style of the flies and their combinations of colors.

When I returned to Holland, I found that information on salmon flies was hard to come by, and obtaining the numerous exotic materials needed to make them was even more difficult. Holland does not have an Atlantic salmon fly tradition, although many of our big rivers, such as the Maas and the Rhine, used to have large runs of salmon in the early 1900s. Most of the salmon fishing was done with nets rather than with rod and line, and because of these historical circumstances, very little information on fly-fishing for salmon was available. Some people I knew in Holland fished elsewhere for salmon but used hair-wing flies, and only a few had full-dressed salmon flies tucked away in their fly wallets.

The next step, I decided, was to research those places which have traditions for tying Atlantic salmon flies. Some of the English and American magazines I bought had articles on salmon flies. I wrote to the authors for information on obtaining the materials needed to tie the flies, and also began to collect salmon fly patterns and books on the subject. By running ads in some of the angling magazines—"Avid flytyer seeks Atlantic salmon fly patterns"—I met so many people that I was devoting one or two nights a week to writing letters. I

wound up corresponding regularly with some eighty tyers around the world, from Tasmania to Nova Scotia, and Norway to Oregon. In the meantime, my collection of books expanded to almost four hundred titles. I was not so much interested in acquiring first editions or inscribed copies as I was in having the books for reference. My collection of patterns grew as well—to almost forty thousand, including streamers and wet and dry flies for trout as well as Atlantic salmon flies.

Two of the first people I wrote were Colin Simpson and Alex Simpson in Scotland. I have piles and piles of Alex's letters written in his small, scribbly handwriting. The writing is so compact that he can fit a paperback's worth of text on a single page of a letter. As I started to tie Atlantic salmon flies, I was unable to find anyone in Holland to help me, so I sent my flies to Alex for his examination. He would return the flies with comments and criticism, and I would then correct the errors and send them back to Alex. The process took a long time but I learned a great deal from him.

It was not until 1988 that I actually met Alex on one of my visits to Scotland. For decades he has been engaged in the enormous task of researching Atlantic salmon fly patterns. He showed me the immense ledger where he records countless patterns, many of which I had never heard of before. The ledger pages, almost two feet wide, are filled with dressings listed in alphabetical order, all in Alex's scribbly handwriting. If a pattern has several dressings, he carefully cross-references them. The dressing for a Green Highlander in one historical book, for example, differs from the dressing for the same fly in another book. When he finds antique salmon flies in old wallets, he analyzes the materials and the pattern and tries to identify the fly by name.

On those early fishing trips to Ireland and Scotland, I used to browse through old tackle shops to find antique hooks

ABOVE:

Royal Lochnagar

or tying materials. My quests were often successful. The local pubs were good sources of information, not only on the fishing in the area but also on local professional and amateur fly dressers. After coming to the same places for a few years, the people got to know me and understood what I was looking for. They would show me fly wallets once owned by their fathers and sometimes tying materials. Most of the time, the flies and materials were suitable only for the garbage bin, but when I got lucky, I would find some blind-eye hooks or usable materials that were otherwise difficult to obtain.

One of the contacts I made was an elderly man from Ireland, Ned McGuire, who was a commercial fly dresser. Since Ned's father was a fly dresser and, in fact, fly dressing went back in his family for four generations, Ned had a wealth of information. He sent me one of the old notebooks in which his father had written down many local patterns and the requests his customers made for specific flies. Ned was pleased to help me because he was very curious about why a young man from a country where there was no salmon fishing was interested in salmon flies.

Suddenly Ned's letters stopped coming. After a while, I received a letter from one of his friends informing me that Ned had passed away. The friend, who had found my correspondence with Ned, kindly wrote me about his death. I contacted the man to ask what had happened to Ned's library and materials. He finally wrote back to tell me that Ned's son had come from the United States to arrange for his father's funeral. Having little time to stay in Ireland and lacking any interest in flytying, the son threw everything away. I was shocked that all the information was gone. This happens all too often, and I feel that fly dressers should find ways to ensure that their knowledge is preserved for the future.

Some of the first flies I tied and sent to Alex Simpson were basic strip-wing flies. I have always liked traditional Spey flies, with their low-set wings and long, flowing hackles of heron and widgeon. Simple and graceful in design, they also appealed to me as effective fish getters. I took a fancy to the Grey Heron, Purple Heron, Black Heron, Culdrain, and many other Spey flies. These very successful flies used in Scotland for centuries have remained virtually unchanged, except for an occasional attempt to use more colorful materials, as in the Delfur Fancy, which combines a married feather wing with the heron hackles. With the revival of interest in Spey flies by con-

temporary American tyers such as Syd Glasso, Dave McNeese, and Bob Veverka, Spey flies have become more colorful and have received the attention they deserve. After I turned to full-dress salmon flies, I became interested in creating my own patterns in the traditional style with traditional materials. Some commemorated a special occasion, such as the birth of a friend's son. For someone who reached retirement, I tied a fly called the Pensioner.

What caused my imagination to run wild was the material that became available from a small mail-order firm with the name of The Kelson Collection. Started in 1989 by a man who had collected birds all his life for taxidermy purposes, the collection gave flytyers access to a wealth of materials never found in salmon fly patterns—feathers from scores of pheasants, parrots, and other unusual birds. These feathers not only served as excellent substitutes for rare materials, such as blue chatterer or Indian crow, but also gave me the opportunity to sit at the tying bench and compose a fly in the classic tradition with feathers that Victorian fly dressers undoubtedly never used. I imagine that in the times of John Younger, James Wright, and George Kelson, fly dressers also made their flies with feathers they had on hand, many of which tyers today would regard as extremely rare.

Dressing my own patterns brought me to the next predicament. Every Atlantic salmon fly has a name. Some, like the Jock Scott and Ferguson, are named after the person who tied the fly or for whom the fly was tied. Salmon flies often honored royalty. There is even a fly of Irish origin named after the Dutch King, William of Orange, better known in Ireland as King Billy. Another very popular practice was to title flies after a stretch of river, like the   RIGHT: *The Macallan* Delfur Fancy, which originated on the Delfur Beat on the Spey in Scotland. So many names have been used that it was difficult to come up with something original. Remembering a sea trout fly called the Glenlivet, I decided to title my "new" patterns after the drink I love the most, malt whisky. There are a few hundred distilleries in Scotland, so I have a while to go before I run out of names—and I hope eventually to sample all the whiskies.

For a long time, I held the reputation of being a salmon fly tyer who had literally hundreds of salmon flies but who had never caught a salmon. Every time I returned from a fishing

trip, someone would ask me if I had caught a salmon. Until very recently, the answer was always negative. My main pursuit was fishing for sea trout. It is possible to hook an Atlantic salmon when casting for sea trout, but this happens very infrequently. Since I do most of my sea trout fishing in Ireland, where the fish are not very big, I use very light tackle. A salmon hooked on light tackle will break off easily.

Fishing for Atlantic salmon has never been my primary interest because it is like playing the lottery. No one knows why salmon take a fly since they do not feed once they leave the ocean and enter the fresh water of a river. I always say that the salmon will catch the fisherman, not the other way around. When fishing for trout, I can try to match the hatch, and for sea trout, I can present a fly that resembles what the fish will take as food, but so far I have never seen a hatch of Green Highlanders with salmon in the feeding lane. Catching an Atlantic salmon is more a matter of being at the right place at the right time, which is very difficult since I live five hundred miles from the nearest place to fish for salmon.

It was luck—being in the right place at the right time—that enabled me to shatter my reputation as a salmon fly tyer who had never caught salmon. In 1987 I went with my family to Ireland, where my father-in-law has a house. We needed to do some shopping, and I was chosen as the volunteer. As I went over the bridge on the way to town, I stopped to do what every fisherman does when crossing a river—I looked down to see if I could spot a few fish. I saw some salmon under the bridge, which is a known lie, especially to local poachers. As I looked at the water, someone tapped me on the shoulder. I turned around, and the man introduced himself as the person who owned the fishing rights on the river. He asked if I wanted to fish the section of river in front of his house.

Abandoning my shopping, I followed him in my car to his house. I took out the only flyrod I had with me—a light trout rod for a number 5 line. I tied on 5x tippet and a sea trout fly called the Slaney Badger, dressed on a small treble hook. I followed my host to the riffle in front of his house. After making a few casts, I felt a sharp tug. The fish put up a brave fight, and as I brought it in, my new friend offered to come to my aid with a net. I declined his help. Slipping a pair of forceps down the line, I released a seven-pound grilse. I have never seen such a horrified look on anyone's face. It turned out that my host had fished the river for over a week and had caught nothing. Later that day, I caught four smaller salmon. The day after, the water rose about two feet and the fishing was completely unproductive. I was left with a new reputation and a story to tell in front of an open fire while smoking a pipe and sipping a lovely old malt.

STEWART CANHAM

There are many theories about why Atlantic salmon flies evolved the way they did, but no one really knows for sure. At some point, the salmon fly started out with a hook and a few bits of fur or feather which had caught a salmon, then progressed all the way to a Jock Scott, the epitome of Atlantic salmon flies. Eventually we wound up with a myriad of fabulous flies. They are so outlandish, crazy really. Why would you want all those materials on a hook? They seem totally unnecessary. A black hair-wing fly will take all the salmon you ever want.

My theory, particularly on full-dress flies, is that the nineteenth century ghillies in Scotland had an unwritten competition about who could get the most materials on a hook in the most beautiful form. I can imagine the conversation among some ghillies in the Victorian age, when salmon fishing was at its height: "Have you seen this fly that so-and-so has just done? Well, I'm going to do a better one than that." As far as I am concerned, the ghillie Jock Scott won the competition, hands down. Maybe the ghillies realized that the flies did not make a crucial difference in catching salmon, and that the more colorful feathers they could get on a hook, the better the sports liked the fly.

Apart from the beauty of full-dress Atlantic salmon flies, the fascination for me is the skill involved in tying them. I tie nearly all feather-wing flies, and marrying feathers for the wings is in itself very satisfying. It might take an hour for me to build a wing, then I quake with suspense wondering if I can tie it on the hook without wrecking it. Is it actually going on the first time? Do I dare let go of the thread to see how it looks? I often go through George Kelson's *The Salmon Fly* to pick out a dressing that requires a lot of hard maneuvers. It is a challenge to be able to tie a complicated fly and come out with a good result at the end of the day. When I have pro-duced a fly that I am satisfied with, then I will choose a new one. I love challenges of all sorts—marrying the feathers for a salmon fly I have never tied before, or fishing under a bush overhanging a stream for a trout that people have walked by all day.

A large proportion of the flies I tie end up being framed. I don't mind. The important part is that I enjoy tying the fly, and that when I have put the whip finish on the head, I am pleased with the result. I have to be in a certain frame of mind to tie Atlantic salmon flies because they require so much intense concentration. I do not like to tie when I feel pressured. Although I am a bit of a perfectionist and want to see my flies improve, there is no point in analyzing the finished fly by picking it to pieces. To me that's taking it too seriously. Being constantly dissatisfied with the end result would drive me insane. If you see a fault, does that guarantee the next fly you tie is going to be better? The nineteenth century tyers who made feather-wing flies for fishing weren't always precise. Did that make their flies any less beautiful or effective?

When I started to tie salmon flies in the late 1970s, I was managing a shop in London, Benwood's Fishing Tackle. It was a real fishing shop. As soon as you came through the door, you started to talk about fishing, and you stopped when you went out. You sat down and had a cup of coffee. There were flies all over the counter. On Saturday afternoons, you couldn't get in the door for all the people drinking coffee and not buying any-thing. I didn't tie flies for the store, but people who knew my trout flies would comment, "Well, you tie great trout flies. Do you tie Atlantic salmon flies?" I had to say no. I thought, "I really should be saying yes. I've got to be able to tie these because they are part of flytying."

At first I didn't know anyone who could teach me how to tie these flies, so I turned to Poul Jorgensen's *Salmon Flies,*

which was the springboard that got me going. He wrote in a way that I could understand and used clear, precise pictures, which makes such a difference when you are learning. After I worked from Jorgensen's book, I moved on to Pryce-Tannatt's. Terry Griffiths, a friend of mine, tied the flies in the third edition of Pryce-Tannatt's *How to Dress Salmon Flies.* He was the first person to give me instruction. It was extremely difficult because Terry is left-handed, and I am right-handed. That was a nightmare, but in the end we solved the problem by watching one another in a mirror.

Once you learn to tie, you have to be guided by books, since they are the only references to the historical tyers and their patterns. To re-create a fly someone else has designed, and to do it properly, I feel you have to be faithful to the way that tyer did it and to the materials that tyer used. If you alter a pattern, then you shouldn't call it a traditional salmon fly. It is not traditional. It is a fly you have designed—a modern design of a traditional salmon fly. If you tie a Jock Scott, then you should tie it as close as possible to the way Jock Scott said it should be tied. That is why I admire Poul Jorgensen. He ties Atlantic salmon flies as he thinks the earlier tyers intended them to be tied. The problem is that the dressings for a pattern may vary from book to book. That worries me because I don't have any idea which author is correct. Did Kelson get the dressing from someone else and change it? Or did the tyer who gave Kelson the dressing change it before Kelson wrote about it? Where is the truth? It is impossible to know.

Running a tackle shop had been a lifelong dream, and when I came to Benwood's in 1976, the fly-fishing boom was just beginning. But old tackle LEFT: **Dusty Miller** was not collected as enthusiastically as it is now. People, especially widows, would bring in antique tackle, sometimes with a box or two of old flies. At first I was interested in the rods and reels, and I was simply given the boxes of flies. I threw away a lot of flies that were damaged by moths. Now I would give my right arm for those hooks. After I started to tie Atlantic salmon flies, I raided some of the old gut-eye flies for the antique hooks.

Of all the surprises that ever happened to me in the shop, the best was buying an extremely rare reel. An Englishman, Alfred Holden Illingworth, who lived at the turn of the century, invented the first fixed spool reel. A furniture maker by trade, he obviously made the reel in his spare time. He produced a limited number of several models and sold them all. They were always very sought-after items. A man who collected reels and lived around the corner from Benwood's used to come in every Saturday. We had a standing joke. I would say, "Yeah, someday I'll find you an Illingworth."

One morning, a lad about ten years old walked in the shop and plunked two boxes on the table. He didn't want to tell me where he got them, and I suspected that he had nicked them. One was a Hardy Perfect, one of the old brass salmon reels. The other, a velvet-lined box, had Illingworth written across the top—brand-new, absolutely immaculate. The reel inside looked as if it had never been touched. "I don't know about this funny old thing," I said, "but I'll give you twenty-five quid for the Hardy." The boy's eyes opened wide. "Twenty-five quid? What about the other one?" "I'll give you a tenner for that," I said, "thirty-five quid for the lot." So he went out the door like a dog with two tails, thinking, "That's the best thing that's ever happened to me." I thought, "I got an Illingworth for a ten." I couldn't believe it. At the time, an Illingworth sold for two to three hundred pounds.

I phoned up my friend at his office and left a message on the answer-phone saying, "I've got your Illingworth." I phoned his home and got his wife. I told her about the Illingworth. It was early December, and she exclaimed, "It's his Christmas present. He'll freak out when I give it to him. He won't believe it." Off she went, and at about four o'clock in the afternoon I suddenly remembered the message I had left on the answer-phone. I panicked and rang up his wife again and told her about the message. She rushed through London to her husband's office, ripped all the tape out of the phone, wrecked about ten important messages, and threw them all in the bin. The only mistake she made was not having a camera on Christmas morning when he opened the present and saw the Illingworth.

I had been involved in the tackle business since I was a teenager. When I was nineteen years old, I took a job at Oliver's of Knebsworth in Hertfordshire, a shop specializing in coarse fishing, which is very popular in England. Ted Oliver's shop was among the very few that produced split-cane rods for coarse fishing, and I wanted to learn how to make them properly. Ted had never been fishing in his life, but he had this uncanny ability of being able to put into a rod an action that suited its purpose. I don't know how he did it. Most people who make tackle are fishermen at heart.

Five miles from the shop lived Richard Walker, probably the greatest English fisherman since Izaak Walton. He was known predominantly for his coarse fishing, though he had tied flies and fished for trout for a long time. Among his achievements, he caught a forty-four-pound carp that held the record in England from 1952 until it was broken in 1985, just before his death. Dick was responsible for the popularity of English reservoir and still-water fishing, which is far more common, available, and affordable than river fishing. He wrote over ten books on fishing and for thirty years had a weekly column in a paper called *Angling Times*. Dick was very controversial. When he wrote a column, he would throw in a comment that made readers write letters to the editor for weeks. He did it intentionally to see what people were thinking. Dick was a very great man.

I had Dick Walker's address and wanted to work up my nerve to knock on his door some evening. He had a reputation for being a bit of an ogre, so I thought, "If he shouts at me, that's okay. I don't mind being shouted at by Dick Walker. I can cope with that." One night after work, I rode my scooter from the shop to his house. I stood outside for about an hour, shaking with anticipation. I finally knocked on the door and waited to see what would happen. The door opened, and there he was. "Yes, can I help you?" I told him who I was and that I was interested in the coarse fishing in the area and he was obviously the man to talk to. He said, "Come in. Have a cup of coffee. Sit down." It was as if we had been friends all along. He had a huge caravan in the garden with all of his fishing tackle in it. We sat out there the rest of the evening as he tied flies and talked about carp fishing. I was interested in the carp fishing, but was mesmerized by watching him tie

flies. I had never seen anybody tie flies before. After that evening, I went to his house one night every week and he showed me the rudiments of flytying.

There was a huge reservoir called Grafham Water up north in Huntingtonshire. In 1966, after the dam was built but before Grafham was opened for fishing, the reservoir was stocked with trout. Within two years, it became such a rich piece of water. The fish were colossal. That first evening I visited Dick Walker, he said, "I'm going to Grafham next week for the opening. Do you want to come with me?" He didn't need to ask more than once. I went—and I have never had a day like that since. We caught five-, six-, and seven-pound rainbows. A phenomenal number of fly lines were lost in the first two weeks Grafham was open because people were fishing with old lines and only about ten yards of backing. One large fish and the line would be gone. It was fabulous.

When I left the area where Dick lived, I was able to visit him only on two occasions. But over the years, we phoned each other frequently. I think one of the best things he did was when I moved with my family to southern England, to the trout farm that we still own. Just before Christmas, someone told him that we had moved, and on Christmas morning, the phone rang and a voice said, "Happy Christmas. How's it going down there?" It was Dick.

I have done all kinds of fishing—coarse fishing for carp, pike, and tench, and fly-fishing for trout, Atlantic salmon, and sea trout—and I like them all. Although in my tying I am a traditionalist, in my fishing I am not a traditionalist for tradition's sake. If a certain method of fishing will catch a fish, then I will use it. But someday, in a river in England, Scotland, or Ireland, I would love to catch a salmon on a traditional Atlantic salmon fly on a blind-eye hook with a gut leader—a fly that I have tied myself.

JIMMY YOUNGER

All my life I have tied flies, and everything I have learned has been through the accumulation of experiences. I was born in a cottage near Kelso on the banks of the River Tweed. The Tweed has the famous Junction Pool, where the River Teviot runs into the River Tweed. About half a mile above the Junction Pool is the Lower Teviot Bridge. Just over that bridge used to sit two cottages, called the Friar's Cottages, which have since been combined into one large house. Our family moved into the first cottage about six months before the outbreak of the Second World War. The cottage had no electricity or running water. Three years later, we were glad to move into a prefab in Kelso with electricity.

My father was a ghillie most of his life. He worked on the Conon, the Naver, the Kirkaig, and the Inver in Scotland. Later in his life, he went to the Welsh Dee and in 1981 came back to Kelso, where he had a part-time job as a ghillie on the Tweed. My father taught me how to fish. He tied flies when he was a boy but he preferred to go fishing. He didn't have the patience for tying. When I was eleven or twelve, I remember going to a small tackle shop in the town of Kelso. The local tyer sat in a little workshop and tied flies, and I sat and watched him. I asked him to teach me tying, but he said he never had the time. He had all these orders for flies, not for hair-wings but for the classic feather-wings. I didn't see hair-wing flies used on the rivers until I moved to the north of Scotland in the early 1960s.

The chap who ran the local shop died very suddenly. The business was sold to Allcock of Redditch and the name changed to Redpath of Kelso. In 1955, when I finished school, my father got me a job there as an apprentice. At that time we were working in Allcock's old premises behind a picture house, a terrible place because it was hot in the summer and freezing in the winter. When Jock MacDougall, who tied the flies, died suddenly in 1956, we moved into his premises, which included a tackle shop and an upstairs flat. The three rooms upstairs were turned into an office, a workroom, and a storeroom. The bottom was a retail shop with clothing and tackle.

When I began as an apprentice, I did not tie flies but spent six months working six days a week from eight in the morning to six in the evening tying bait tackles. A bait tackle was a kind of tandem hook that made a worm look more natural. There were two-hook tackles and three-hook tackles. The front hook had an eye for attaching to the leader. The other was a blind-eye hook with a tapered shank. The hooks had to be tied together, then varnished. I hung the finished tackles on a length of nylon stretched between two pieces of wood at my tying bench. On Fridays I stopped tying a little early and gathered all of the tackles so that they could be counted. I was paid by the piece. That was my introduction to flytying.

When I actually went on to tie flies, I made Spiders. I teased wool and dubbed it on the hook for the body and had to learn to tie on double feather hackles. I almost cried because I was unable do it. When tyers could double the hackles, they could make a spider in half the time—and I was still doing piecework. I finally mastered it. The same happened with the whip finish. I couldn't understand it at first, but each week I would progress. I tied Spiders for a week, then went on to such wet flies as the March Brown, Greenwell's Glory, and Teal and Silver, and many others. If I made the fly wrong, I always cut it off the hook with a pen knife and saved the hook.

The man at the Redpath factory who taught me to tie was a great flytyer, though no one knows about him. He was also a great teacher. His name was John French Muir. He was named after a naval captain, John French, and his nickname was Frenchie. He had joined the factory as a boy. He worked up until the war, went to war, was captured the first day he landed in Germany, and spent the war at a camp as a prisoner

ABOVE, CLOCKWISE FROM
TOP LEFT:

Munro Killer
Garry Dog
Dusty Miller
Watson's Fancy
Arndilly Fancy
Black Doctor

of war. He never even fired a gun and after the war, in 1946, returned to the job. John never married. All he did was fish for salmon and tie flies and walk. He walked and walked and walked—he never owned a bicycle or a motorcar.

When I was almost seventeen, I moved to Glasgow to work in a tackle shop, William Robertson and Company on Wellington Street, owned by Colin and Angus Robertson. It was my first time away from home, and to me Glasgow was a big city. At that time, I had another profession, as a jazz drummer in a band. I had studied piano as a boy, and when I went to Glasgow, I attended the school of music a couple nights a week to learn percussion. To earn a living, I played two or three nights a week and tied flies during the day. I had become a good trout fly tyer and had even tied simple salmon flies, not for sale but for my father to fish with. In 1960, I turned professional and worked as a drummer for six years. I met my wife Gloria when I was booked to play at her twenty-first birthday party. I didn't have enough time to tie flies professionally, but later had to stop playing the drums when I hurt my back. My back got worse and worse, and for four or five months I was in a plaster cast.

My father was working in Loch Inver. The man who ran the hotel there was a very famous fisherman, Charles C. McLaren. McLaren wrote books on salmon and sea trout and was the world's best amateur caster. McLaren bought the Altnaharra Hotel, another very famous hotel for fishers, on Loch Navar. I asked him for work because the cast I wore for my back made it impossible for me to sit for long periods. He gave me a job as a barman. I looked after two bars, the public and the residents'. The residents' bar was quiet all day because the guests were out fishing. I set up a vise at the bar counter and sat on a high stool. I tied flies during the day and sold them at night.

When the cast was removed and my job was about to

end, a guest in the hotel who came from Golspie in the north of Scotland said he was starting a flytying factory, Sutherland Fly, in Helmsdale, north of Brora, and asked me to manage it. I took the job, but Gloria and I couldn't find a place to live in Helmsdale, so we moved to Brora, which is only six or seven miles south. We rented a cottage, an old coast-guard house, with walls about three feet thick, right off the estuary of the Brora River. I could cast a line out the window into the estuary. I met Megan Boyd through Gloria because they had known one another through Scottish country dancing. We lived only a mile or two from Megan's bungalow north of Brora. On my way home from the factory in Helmsdale in the evening, I frequently stopped by to visit and tie flies beside Megan. Once in a while, when she was behind in her orders, I tied flies for her stock.

My job at Sutherland Fly was to teach tyers. We put ads in the local papers: Flytyers wanted, no experience necessary, will teach. We hired about twenty people, mostly women, for the factory to tie both trout and salmon flies. Sutherland Fly produced thousands of flies that were exported to the United States and Canada—Silver, Black, Gray, and Rusty Rats, Cossebooms. We occasionally had so much work to do that we subcontracted some of the orders to Megan in the winter when her business was slow after the fishing season closed.

When I lived in Brora, I won a flytying competition sponsored in 1969 by the Fly Dressers' Guild. I tied a full-dress feather-wing fly and named it for Prince Philip, who came to Glasgow in 1969 to open a Scottish craft exhibition. The colors I chose for the fly match the purple and gold of the royal cloak. A man who knew I had won the award called me out of the blue: "Do you want to go to Hong Kong?" I considered it for about a week and accepted. Gloria and I lived in the Far East for seven years, from 1969 to 1976. I managed a factory in Hong

Kong, the International Fly Dressing Corporation. The factory had about sixty tyers. There was also a branch in Macao. Most of the flies we tied were for trout and steelhead and were exported to the United States and Canada. We also tied bucktails for coho fishing off the Vancouver coast of Canada.

After returning to Scotland, Gloria and I tied for our own shop in Durness on the north coast opposite the Orkney Islands. The season there is very short, from the middle of May to the middle of September, when all the tourists go home. We tied all year because we relied on selling flies for our livelihood. We could write a book about the people we met on the north coast. Many of them had been coming to the area since they were children, and their parents had also fished the same places ever since they were children. The long winters up north were the primary reason we decided to move south in 1980 to the Dumfries area.

For years we supplied large companies such as Hardy and Farlow. Our flies were sold as their flies, so no one knew we had made them. The first year we tied on our own was 1990. Very few professional tyers make salmon flies full-time. We tie the more standard patterns used on the rivers in Scotland, England, Ireland, Norway, and Iceland for salmon as well as sea trout: hair-wings, shrimp, General Practitioners, low-water patterns, tube flies, flies on Waddington hooks. The first hair-wings I ever tied were sizes 6, 8, and 10. Only in the last two years have we started to tie size 12s, and that was for fishing in Iceland when the water was very low. Now in this country, people are also using 12s. People request full-dress flies but I rarely tie them. Tyers have invented many patterns for exhibition and for fishing, and in my life I have seen flies evolve from the classic feather-wings to the hair-wings, and even the hair-wings have become simpler and simpler. I have tied tens of thousands of flies and have tied for so long that it is almost automatic. I just like tying and fishing, and I have met so many interesting people.

KEN SAWADA

TOKYO, JAPAN

Japan has its own fly-fishing traditions that go back a hundred years or more. For fishing in fresh water, there were two kinds of flies. Small, very colorful flies that looked like nymphs were fished for *ayu*, which resemble grayling. The other type were very simple flies for trout. Tied on size 6, 8, and 10 hooks, they looked like worms or nymphs. The bodies were made of cotton thread or the floss from a mountain fern. The hackles were of sparrow or pheasant feathers. Some commercial fishermen used these Japanese-style flies to fish for *iwana*, a species of trout, as well as for *yamame*, a landlocked salmon. The rod was a bamboo pole, not split cane, and did not have a reel. The line was of horse-hair. These early flies were very primitive compared with the artificial flies that most tyers dress today.

Trout fishing became more common in Japan after World War II. Many people fished with bait, but some enjoyed the traditional form of Japanese fly-fishing. Modern fly-fishing methods were introduced to Japan after the war. The Americans who stayed in Japan, and those who moved here, also began to fish for trout, and they ordered flies made of fur and feathers from Japanese flytyers. The Japanese knew little about fly-fishing or about why they should tie a fly a certain way, but eventually their flies were imported for sale in the tackle shops in the United States. In Japan today, fly-fishing on streams and tying flies are very popular. There are very few professional flytyers, but most Japanese anglers are very good at tying their own flies.

I began to tie flies shortly after I opened my tackle business in 1968. I had seen pictures of flies in English angling books and was interested in dressing dry flies for trout. At that time, quality materials and tools for tying flies were hard to find in Japan. For the first fly I tied, I plucked the plumes from a feather duster. The only tying instructions I had read were in a Japanese magazine and were for making traditional Japanese flies without using tools. After learning about Veniard Ltd. in England, I started to order hooks, materials, and tools through the mail. Using John Veniard's *Fly Dresser's Guide*, I taught myself how to tie flies and worked steadily to improve my tying. Initially I was interested in fishing with dry flies because it was so exciting to cast to rising trout rather than to follow the Japanese method of fishing with wet flies. But many people told me that it would be impossible to fish with dry flies in the Japanese streams. Japan is a mountainous country, and many rivers are very fast flowing and the fish are very wary. I decided to dress very bushy dry flies with twice as much hackle so that the flies would be very buoyant in the water. I succeeded in catching many fish using heavily dressed flies in such patterns as the Quill Gordon, Royal Coachman, and Black Gnat. Then I invented some light-colored flies, in white and cream, that I could see in the rapid water of the mountain streams.

In the early 1970s, I made two trips to Europe. In 1972, I went to Scotland, where I first fished for Atlantic salmon, on the River Tay. I fished for only two days and caught two salmon. I was very lucky. In Japan, the only kinds of salmon that we are allowed to fish for as a sport are the cherry salmon, the *sakura masu*, and the *yamame*, the landlocked cherry salmon. The cherry salmon is a very beautiful name for a very beautiful fish. These salmon are named for the cherry blossoms that bloom in the early spring, when the fish swim up the rivers from the Sea of Japan and the Pacific Ocean. Cherry salmon are silvery, like a coho, and their eyes are very unusual, like those of an eagle. The average size is five or six pounds, up to fifteen. Other salmon come upriver right before spawning, but cherry salmon enter the fresh water in February, March, and April, and do not spawn until September, October, or November. Unlike the Atlantic salmon, the cherry salmon always die after spawning.

Although I love fishing for cherry salmon, it took me three years to catch my first one. Spin casters can easily catch cherry salmon, but it is very difficult to catch them on a fly. As I experimented with flies for cherry salmon, I invented one called the Aquamarine, which looks like a streamer and combines pink and dark blue bucktail, polar bear hair, and shimmering man-made fibers in the wing, tied over a body of silver Mylar piping. The cheeks of the fly are blue peacock neck feathers, with jungle cock eyes. The Aquamarine turned out to be the most successful of all the flies I tied. It was so effective that many Japanese fly-fishers started to fish it for cherry salmon.

In 1974, I decided to go to Europe to learn more about fly-fishing and fly-tying. My first destination was England, where I met John Veniard. I showed him the trout flies I had tied and he gave me many useful hints and techniques. I did not have much time to fish in England because I was going next to France to meet Charles Ritz. I learned about Ritz from a friend of mine in Japan. When I mentioned to this friend that I wanted to know more about fly casting, he told me about a friend of his, Arnold Gingrich, who had been the editor of *Esquire* magazine and knew a very famous fly caster. When I read Ritz's book, *A Fly Fisher's Life*, I was fascinated by the photographs of him casting, but was unable to understand how he could cast a fly line so far with such an elegant, restrained style. Most casters I had seen looked as if they were throwing a javelin at a track meet. I wrote Ritz at his hotel and he suggested that I visit him in Paris.

I was in Paris for four days. The first day I was there it rained. The second day it rained. The third day it rained and was very windy. On the fourth day, it only rained lightly. I called Ritz and he said, "Today is a nice day," and told me to meet him at the hotel. From there we went to the famous park, the Bois de Boulogne, to a pond called Tir au Pigeon, where casting tournaments used to be held. Ritz brought many split-cane and fiberglass rods with him. Some were prototypes he had designed. Others were production models. We spent only three hours together, but in the brief time I watched Ritz cast, I saw that his casting stroke was very short and involved a very little motion. Ritz handed me one of his rods, and after he instructed me for thirty minutes, I could cast a fly line more beautifully than I ever could before. I didn't know why. "Now that you can cast," Ritz told me, "you have to practice." I knew

he was right, and six months after I returned to Japan, I was able consistently to cast a line with a beautiful form, very fast, like a rocket.

Although I have been tying flies for twenty years, I did not start tying Atlantic salmon flies until 1986. When I read the old books, such as those by George Kelson, T. E. Pryce-Tannatt, and Francis Francis, I saw that they contained many patterns for salmon flies but few illustrations, and that most of the illustrations were very small and unclear. The best way I could see the flies was to tie them myself. As I dressed more and more flies, I became able to picture a fly in my mind before I tied the pattern. The more interested I became in salmon flies, the more I wanted to do a book showing the beauty of these flies. My first book on Atlantic salmon flies, *Salmon Fly Dressing*, was an instructional book with step-by-step color photographs. After it came out in 1989, I continued to dress Atlantic salmon flies, hoping to tie one hundred or one hundred fifty, if possible two hundred, for another book. But after reading many historical books with so many dressings, I reached five hundred flies and decided that would be the number I would include in my next book. I thought that, if I wanted to see so many patterns, other fly-tyers would, too. When I saw different Japanese books with beautiful color pictures of jewels, ancient tools, traditional cloths, and other objects, I imagined making the same kind of book for Atlantic salmon flies.

In early 1989, after I had tied two or three hundred salmon flies, I received a letter from Paul Schmookler, who sent me pictures of two of his original flies, the Double Leopard and the Indian Summer. Looking at his flies was as inspirational to my flytying as looking at the photograph of Charles Ritz was to my casting. Paul's Atlantic salmon flies were different from others I had seen. Before that moment, I didn't know whether or not I could dress my own patterns, but when I saw Paul's flies, I decided I could. I was so excited about inventing my own designs that I dressed the first nine flies in one week. I tied a total of forty-two original patterns in two months. When I made the final selection of flies for *The Art of the Classic Salmon Fly*, I eliminated forty-two of the five hundred traditional patterns I felt were very similar to some of the other classic flies I had tied to make room for my new designs.

I worked very hard over two years to tie the five hundred

patterns in my book. Some of the flies took me three hours to tie, without changing them from the image I had in my mind. As I tied other flies, I modified them and they took longer to complete. For each pattern in the book, I tied only one fly—there is no spare—and I sometimes used substitute materials for the left side of the wings, or omitted the materials from the left side, knowing that the flies were to be photographed, not to be fished. When I tied the traditional patterns, I first visualized the order of colors in the married wings. Because many patterns call for similar color combinations with too many contrasts, I occasionally rearranged the sequence of colors to make the married wings more pleasing and elegant. In my own patterns, I wanted simple color combinations, and many have only two or three colors, or colors that are very close in value.

In creating my original patterns, I followed two processes. When I saw particular materials, I arranged them in my mind into a fly with harmonious shapes. My mind became like the screen of a computer to which I added the color graphics. After I painted the fly in my mind, I sat down to tie it. The inspiration for other flies came from a photograph, a painting, or another image that I liked. I tried to transfer the colors or other elements in the image into my flies. I was always thinking about creating new patterns, not only when I sat at my tying desk, but when I was driving a car or relaxing with a cup of coffee. To remember some of the patterns, I drew them on paper.

Sometimes I chose the title of a fly when I invented the pattern. For other flies, I changed the name two or three times as I searched for the best title to reflect the qualities or mood of the fly. I always wanted to tie a fly that reminded me of dawn and the rising sun. The first fly of the forty-two I originated was Daybreak, which I tied one day after seeing the sunrise. I dressed the fly named Ecstasy after I saw the painting titled *Ecstasy* by Maxfield Parrish. When I created Blizzard, I was remembering the high mountains in early spring. In my book, my own Atlantic salmon flies have captions in both Japanese and English, but the Japanese names have more than one translation. I used the name Un-Married Angel, for example, for a fly with a wing that is not made of married feathers. The Japanese name also literally means a woman who has never been married. The Japanese name for the fly I titled Stardust translates as "dream of midsummer night." Reflection also means "water temptations," and Memories means "meeting again."

A few people who saw my book of five hundred Atlantic salmon flies wondered why I would take the time to dress so many of these patterns because fish often take flies that are not so beautiful. Many other people told me they never imagined that fishing flies could be so special. It is true that fish will take many kinds of flies, some of them beautiful, some of them not. I love fly-fishing and flytying so much that, when I open my fly box, I always want to pick out a beautiful fly to cast to a fish.

ABOVE:

Daybreak

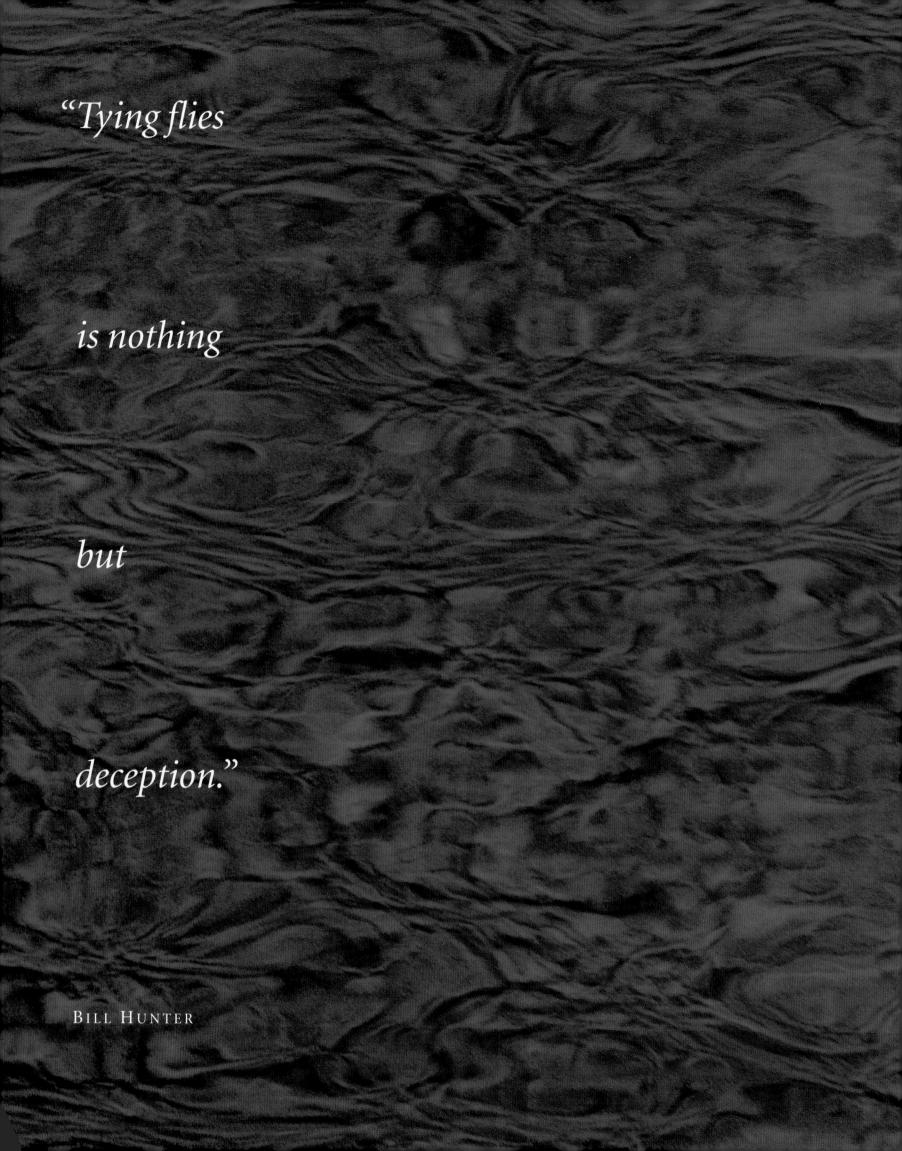

"Tying flies

is nothing

but

deception."

BILL HUNTER

Eastern
United States

POUL JORGENSEN

Blue Rat

Durham Ranger

Sir Conrad

MIKE MARTINEK

Mike's Red Ghost Special

Royal Marine

BOB VEVERKA

Three-Eyed Monster

Tri-Color Spey

CHARLIE KROM

Blue Doctor

Copper Killer

Gold Fever

Helmsdale Doctor

Silver Monkey

PAUL SCHMOOKLER

Comet

Double Leopard

BILL HUNTER

Black Doctor

Green Highlander

Jock Scott

KEITH FULSHER

Reynard Series

RON ALCOTT

Colonel's Lady

Jock Scott

POUL JORGENSEN

One of my foremost interests is to make sure that history is not forgotten and is passed on to other generations. I guess the older we get, the more we start to think about posterity. This art can be traced back several centuries, and many of the early designs for Atlantic salmon flies have been carried through all these years until the present. The Atlantic salmon fly has come so far, and its traditions deserve to be continued into the future.

I want to perpetuate these traditions in my tying, teaching, and writing. I believe in following traditional dressings for Atlantic salmon flies and the methods for tying them. If you are trying to copy flies that originated in the Victorian era, you need to follow them as exactly as possible—or you should come up with an entirely new concept or style. I don't think that we are ready for such a dramatic departure, and the truth is that very few tyers today do not tie the classics. Although I experiment in the privacy of my tying room, I still describe myself as a traditionalist. The day may come, however, when the lack of important materials will cause tyers to make changes or substantial modifications in salmon fly patterns.

I continue to read about history, and I talk about tradition in my classes. Students need to know the origins of Atlantic salmon tying. I did not invent it—there were generations before me. I teach the traditional methods, but I do not put a leash on the people in a class by saying that they shouldn't use their own imaginations. On the contrary, I encourage them to think for themselves. Whatever students do afterward with their knowledge is up to the individual. Once students learn the basics and can tie traditional patterns, then they can go on to other styles. But you must learn the basics, no matter what fly you're tying.

My mother was a piano teacher. My two sisters learned the piano and I learned to play violin. We had one thing in common—the scale. We had to start with the scale before we went into classical music, or jazz, or any other style. The same is true in flytying: You start with the basics, tie trout flies or salmon flies, then develop your own style. People come up to me and say, "But my flies don't look like yours." My response is, "Why should they? You're not tying to make flies that look like mine." The important thing is that you are pleased with the flies and enjoy what you are doing, not that the flies look like someone else's. Not everybody has a creative mind and artistic abilities, but everybody can learn to tie a fly to fish with, because the fish aren't concerned if the tail of a fly is too long. If the fly looks like something to eat, the fish will take it. They do not count the windings of thread or look to see if the material is natural or synthetic, or the hook is English or Japanese.

When I started to tie flies, I learned the basics from Bill Blades. I met him in 1955, after I had moved to the United States from South America. I lived in Glenview, near Chicago, and about forty-five miles north was a chain of lakes that offered good fishing. I had been fly-fishing for several years but had never tied flies. One day I went to Diamond Lake. Out on the lake was a man sitting in a boat. I watched him row to shore and enter the nearby coffee shop. I followed him—he was the only one there—and asked if I could join him. He introduced himself as Bill Blades, and I suppose he was a little astonished that I did not know who he was. After we finished and left the coffee shop, I helped him put his gear in the car.

He opened the trunk and I saw what I thought were insects that he had been collecting. He told me they were artificial flies. I looked at them, amazed, because they were so different from the flies I bought at the store by the lake. He told me he had written a book several years before about how

OPPOSITE:

Sir Conrad

to make these flies. I knew I had to have that book. I paid him for the book and he later brought a signed copy of *Fishing Flies and Fly Tying* to my house. I purchased a vise and some materials, and started to tie using his book. I came to a part that I didn't understand, but it took me a couple of weeks to get up the nerve to call him. I had never met anyone who had written books and was very nervous. But when I called Bill, he invited me to his house in Wilmette. I spent an evening with him, and he showed me all kinds of things in his tying room. That was the beginning of a seven-year friendship.

At the time, I was working as an engineer, and flytying became a hobby. Bill continued to help me, and I went through his school of thought, which meant that I became an apprentice. He showed me a rooster neck. Then he held out a razor blade. "This razor blade is very important," he said. "Every time you put a feather or another material on the hook that I don't like, you can use the razor blade to take it off." It was a long time before I even finished a fly, because he was a perfectionist and wanted me to practice every step until I got it right.

As I went through his book, I was intrigued by the pictures of Atlantic salmon flies. Being a mechanical engineer, I was fascinated that anyone could take feathers and make them sit the way they were supposed to. I thought they were beautiful artistic creations. I asked Bill where I could get more information on salmon flies. He said, "You won't need it." "I don't know about that," I answered. He said, "You're not ready to do

an Atlantic salmon fly. It will be quite a while before I'll even talk to you about salmon flies." He finally did start to tell me about them, but unfortunately he died in 1962. We weren't finished yet. I had such a tremendous respect for Bill — I really thought he was god in disguise—that I never showed him any of the flies I was working on in the privacy of my tying room. With the lessons I had from Bill and from watching him tie, I decided to tie Atlantic salmon flies on my own. I kept practicing after his death, and at the end of the 1960s I quit my job and went into tying professionally.

At first, the only way I thought I could make a living in this business was tying for people who went fishing. So I tied for some of the better-known salmon anglers. Ernest Schwiebert took people to Iceland to fish for Atlantic salmon and sent them to me for flies. Then one day I was demonstrating Atlantic salmon flies for a shop in Washington, D.C. I was paid a fee of fifty dollars, which was a lot then. That afternoon, a Japanese woman came up to me and put twenty-five dollars on the table where I was tying. She said, "I'd like you to tie a fly for me." I tied a full-dress fly for her and she gave me the twenty-five dollars. I thought that was very interesting—if she was willing to pay that much for a fly, others would be, too. So every time I tied at the angling shows, I brought along some salmon flies in little boxes. When someone asked me how much they were, I said twenty-five dollars. I sold all of them.

After I made the leap from tying fishing flies for two dollars apiece, the interest of collectors came gradually, and little by little, I got smart and raised the prices. Nowadays, it is not that my flies are superior to anyone else's, but the name I can sign to them is desirable to collectors. That day in Washington I knew I had crossed the line into a different realm and wanted to concentrate on Atlantic salmon flies. Salmon fly anglers and collectors today are knowledgeable, though they may not be able to tie their own flies. They know exactly how many layers of feathers should be in a particular fly. If any are missing, they will remind you.

I tie many classic salmon fly patterns, such as the Durham Ranger, which appeared on the cover of my third book, and occasionally I am asked to design a fly for a special occasion or specific area of fishing. This may seem unwarranted since the array of known flies covers a wide spectrum of colors and range of patterns. Nonetheless, I designed the Blue Rat in 1977, as an addition to the Rat series, specifically for fishing in Iceland, where flies with blue seem to take more fish than other flies do. The Blue Rat has been fished with great success on the Laxi i Kjos and Nordura rivers in Iceland. Considered as good as the Blue Charm, it also works well on most rivers in North America. The Sir Conrad is another fly I am known for. Designed in the mid-1970s for actor William ("Cannon") Conrad, the original was dressed on a 7/0 ten-karat, gold-plated hook and framed as a gift to the actor from the *American Sportsman* television show.

After a number of years tying and teaching, I thought that writing a book about Atlantic salmon flies needed

BELOW:

Blue Rat

to be done. I had already published two books. In the first, *Dressing Flies for Fresh and Salt Water*, I touched on Atlantic salmon flies, chiefly hair-wings. When I began to tie salmon flies, it was hard to find literature on the subject. George Kelson's *The Salmon Fly* and T. E. Pryce-Tannatt's *How to Dress Salmon Flies* had not yet been reissued. Bill Blades's *Fishing Flies and Fly Tying* did not go into Atlantic salmon flies in depth. Joseph Bates's *Atlantic Salmon Flies & Fishing* contained many patterns and useful information on the patterns, but no instructions on tying. When my book, *Salmon Flies: Their Character, Style, and Dressing*, came out in 1978, it was the first new book in sixty years devoted entirely to the subject.

Initially I had trouble selling the book to a publisher. I wrote an outline and sent it to Stackpole Books, which had been eager for me to do another book. The people at Stackpole liked the outline, but had already made an agreement with Lee Wulff for a book on Atlantic salmon fishing. The publisher told me they had done a survey indicating that only twenty-five hundred people fish for salmon regularly. I told them they had misunderstood my intentions because I was not catering to salmon anglers but to the quarter million flytyers who were very anxious to have something new to work with. The outline was returned to me. Two weeks later, an editor called me and said, "How fast can you get that outline back to us?" I sent it right back and shortly thereafter signed a contract to do the book. The publisher had decided there was room for two books. I was very happy about that.

The patterns in *Salmon Flies*, from hair-wing flies to strip-wings and feather-wings, are part of an established line of flies that have been carried through the generations. I made some changes in the earlier tying methods, and I contributed my own style of tying, which reflects what I learned from Bill Blades and the influence of Pryce-Tannatt. My book started several things that I can put my finger on. It offered a new avenue of tying by providing encouragement and instruction for all those tyers who had always wanted to tie salmon flies but did not know where to find the information. Once they had read my book, they began looking for the earlier books and for the materials. That was a big step.

In the 1970s, materials such as chatterer, bustard, toucan, Indian crow, and heron were difficult to obtain. In my book, all I could do was give a description of the actual material and recommend a substitute. When the interest in Atlantic salmon flies blossomed, tyers started discovering sources for these materials. As a substitute for seal's fur, I came up with Seal-Ex in the mid-1970s. Originally it was for nymphs, but some of the colors were ideal for salmon flies. Tyers who teach should be aware that many people still cannot obtain certain feathers or may find them too expensive. The average person who is interested in flytying as a recreational pursuit needs to know about substitutes or will be unable to tie an Atlantic salmon fly.

There is one book I have yet to do—a book on realistic flies. It's going to be a tough book to write. The realistic flies I tie are very much in demand, and making them requires a special kind of discipline. They are very unforgiving because they attempt to duplicate an insect. It is, however, impossible to duplicate nature or create an exact imitation of an insect, but it is feasible to make a close study of it. Knowing the anatomy of the insect is essential. If you are a sculptor trying to represent a human being and you have made an arm that is a little too long, a leg that is a little too short, or a head that is too big in proportion to the rest of the body, your work is inadequate. Correct proportions are as crucial to realistic flies, and to salmon flies, as they are to that sculpture.

Many people would like to tie realistic flies, but few are willing to invest the time. My realistic mayfly represents over thirty years of constantly looking for new and different materials and trying out new techniques to achieve the final product. It wasn't until six years ago that I added another pair of wings. I have one particular fly that I have spent ten years on and, as yet, have not come up with a satisfactory solution. As I have stated many times, flytying is a school from which we never graduate. I am sure that I will never graduate because every time I tie a fly I learn something new. I still practice two or three hours a day, without even tying a fly. I manipulate a feather. I try a new technique or take notes. I am doing new things all the time. They may not materialize into a fly but I practice them over and over. Sometimes they go in the wastebasket and I start all over again. Finally, I come up with a fly worth saving.

There are two reasons why people never learn to tie flies, no matter how hard they try. They fail to follow instructions and they are unwilling to practice. The need to practice is one of the first points I emphasize in every class. Some people take my classes six or seven times, and they are novices when they come back. I ask them, "When was the last time you practiced?" They say, "Oh, about six or seven months ago. I thought I needed a refresher course." My answer is "You need a refresher course every day of your life."

Tying artistic flies is important to me for one reason. It may not be the same for everybody, but flytying has always given me an escape and an outlet. For a long time, I thought I was seeking something that I could control. I now know that I have little control over tying a fly. For me, flytying is actually a form of therapy that keeps me sane. When I sit down and tie flies, it's impossible to talk to me. I ignore everything around me and become completely absorbed. As I tie flies, I am not alone. Bill Blades is always sitting next to me in spirit. Sometimes I explain all the new materials to him. I wish that he could be here to try them out. When young people learn enough to tie flies, I hope that some of them will teach and pass on the traditions. I like to think that when I am long gone, someone will say, "I learned from Poul Jorgensen." If I don't leave anything else, I would like to leave that.

MIKE MARTINEK

STONEHAM, MASSACHUSETTS

The landlocked salmon is a spectacular, rare jewel of a game fish found in mysterious, out-of-the-way lakes lined with spruce and dotted with loons. There is an eternal magic of being in a boat out on the water in the early morning when ground fog and mist still hover on the lake, of peeling off line and making sure the fly is swimming correctly, then committing the fly to the depths. There is something special about the peacefulness of the surroundings and the quiet tones of boat conversation. That feeling of tranquility is shattered instantly by the strike of a salmon, the screaming of the reel as the fish runs, and the bending of the rod as I try to gain a little bit on the fish and see how big it is as soon as I can bring it close to the boat. I have never lost the wonderment and delight that go along with that experience.

Landlocked salmon are extremely game. A landlocked caught on light tackle on a streamer early in the season or in the fall strikes savagely and unpredictably. The landlocked shares its thoroughbred fighting heart with its river-born counterpart and tends to behave very much like an Atlantic salmon of the same size. The fish jumps spectacularly and takes out line for long runs. It does not give up easily, and you often lose it when it jumps.

The term "landlocked" is somewhat erroneous because, in most cases, the fish has had the option to vacate the lake system in which it is found, but for some reason has elected to stay. Perhaps the original fish were fatigued or had insufficient biological imprinting that would make them continue beyond the lake system to smaller tributaries to spawn. Whatever the reason, over the years a significant portion of fish remained behind in large lakes in New England and Canada and found an environment where they could forage, feed, and spawn successfully. Because of this adaptation, the landlocked salmon, or lake Atlantic salmon, originally named *Salmo salar sebago*,

has developed certain color, shape, and size characteristics that differ slightly from those of the parent species, though it is still the same fish.

In certain lakes, such as Sebago Lake in Maine, one of the most famous landlocked salmon fisheries in the world, landlocked salmon were caught from the Civil War period through the early 1900s, the peak of the fishery. Salmon weighing fifteen to twenty pounds were not unknown, and the largest fish taken from Sebago was a twenty-two-and-one-half pound salmon, caught in the early 1900s. Because of fishing pressure and the cyclic fortune of fish in lakes, it is unlikely that a fish of that size will ever be caught there again. Now a seven-pound landlocked is very large.

Although I have caught landlocked salmon on dry flies, wet flies, and small streamers in streams and rivers, the chances of covering a lot of water and therefore maximizing the opportunities of catching large fish are best when using a fly rod and a streamer on a lake in the spring, early in the season. Streamers work so well because they have an animation in the water that causes them to swim like baitfish. The color of some streamers may seem farfetched when you look at the fly in your hand or in a fly box. But the flies are often fished twenty feet down in the water and are trolled at four to five miles per hour while being quickly tugged and jerked. The streamer and the landlocked salmon are irrevocably linked.

What the fish sees is purely speculative to people, but the colors of the materials in the fly blend together and look more fishy than the fly-fisher is aware of. Certain colors—pure yellow, white, red, orange, and green—are attractor colors. Nevertheless, the impressionistic entity that the salmon sees is of a fish, whether or not it has the exact tonalities of a smelt, which is a grayish green or silver. Smelt also vary from lake to lake. In Sebago, they are purply blue on the back with silver sides. I have seen smelt in New Hampshire lakes with a sandy green, almost brownish back and a somewhat transparent quality. Smelt in Vermont lakes verge on lavender and pink.

My interest in fishing began when I was a young boy. The father of my best friend Steve Andrick was a taxidermist, as well as a fisherman and hunter. Steve and I began to fashion many crude creations using feathers plucked from his father's surplus stuffed-bird collection. Asthma forced Steve into early retirement, but I persisted, devouring all available magazines and books on the subject of fly-fishing. The old Herter's guide became dog-eared with use. Although I learned to tie all kinds of flies, I was enamored of the grace and beauty of streamer flies.

As I began to find out more about streamers, I realized that certain kinds are unique to New England. Some type of streamer was probably developed in the nineteenth century in Great Britain, but at the turn of the century, New England flytyers refined it and made it their own. I then became interested in regional patterns and why a pattern worked in some locales and not in others. I tracked down and cataloged unusual patterns or patterns that I had not seen before.

I studied original examples of early classic Maine flies by Gardner Percy, Herb Welch, A. W. Ballou, and Chief Needahbeh, who represented various parts of the state. Percy tied flies for his own company, Percy Tackle, which supplied flies to sporting camps throughout Maine. Welch, who lived at Haines' Landing on Lake Mooselookmeguntic, came up with the Black Ghost, which is probably one of the top streamer flies ever tied. Ballou was from Duxbury, Massachusetts, and is given credit as the first person to experiment with marabou as a flytying material. Chief Needahbeh, a Penobscot Indian guide, fished the Moosehead Lake region in Maine and tied big gaudy flies. He invented the flat-wing or biplane streamer.

But of all the tyers I researched, I was most influenced by Carrie Stevens's style of tying, her sense of proportion, and her elements of construction. When I was in my early twenties, I was tying flies at a meeting of the United Flytyers in Boston. A scholarly looking man in his early sixties came up to me and gazed at what I was tying. "You're not tying some of these flies the way they should be tied," he said. "You can fish with them, but that Gray Ghost, for example, is not tied the way it was originally tied." I was floored because I thought that my

version of Stevens's best-known fly was as good as any of the other interpretations I had ever seen.

The man was Austin Hogan, and at the next meeting, he brought in a Gray Ghost and several other flies tied by Stevens. Although her flies varied, I was immediately drawn to the slick, low, swept-back wing on her streamers. The best ones had a very defined proportion and shape lacking in many other flies I had seen, which by comparison seemed awkward and static. Other streamers might assume a certain shape and silhouette in the water that could attract a fish, but they didn't look like a baitfish, and they didn't look aerodynamic, as if they were meant to swim. Flies by Stevens, and flies by a few other tyers too, appear waterborne, even when they are dry.

For years I had tried to achieve this effect in my flies, and Austin helped me with criticism and encouragement. He was unflinchingly direct, even cruel, in his comments, but every once in a while, I would tie a fly that merited his approval. Austin was extraordinarily well informed about the history of every aspect of American tying and fly-fishing and its sources in Great Britain. I have met no one else in my life who possesses even half of the information that Austin did. During the time I knew him, he acquired Carrie Stevens's notes from Wendell Folkins, who had purchased Stevens's business after she retired in 1952. Although Austin died in 1985, he will always be looking over my shoulder as I tie.

Stevens spent most of her time living at a camp in Upper Dam, Maine, located between Lake Mooselookmeguntic and Richardson Lake in the Rangeley Lakes region. Her husband Wallace was a guide. She tied flies actively from 1925 to 1953 and is remembered primarily for her streamers and for some innovative bucktail patterns. Many other types of flies she probably invented are forever lost because no one saved them.

Stevens pioneered a particular style of streamer fly that surfaced early in the century in New England.

Around 1900, some sort of elongated flies, or streamers, were adapted from English flies and fished in the United States. I have a circa 1907 brochure from a sporting camp called Ball's Camp on Grand Lake Stream in Maine, which at that time was one of the best places in the world to fish for landlocked salmon. The brochure describes the fishing, the amenities, and the daily rates. The last page tells what to bring on a trip. The flies listed are what we would recognize today as large wet flies, mostly of British origin and tied on large hooks for lake fishing, often called "lake flies." They are attractive, but they don't look like baitfish. At the bottom of the last page is a very cryptic little sentence in italic: "Be sure to ask our guides about the sensational new white feather."

This gives me a good inkling that a flytyer had taken white hackles from a mattress or quilt and tied them to a hook. Or perhaps a wet fly became so beat up after repeated use that the hackle unwound and trailed behind the hook, and the fly took even more fish. According to one story, after World War I, in the Grand Lake area, someone started using feathers from a boat cushion to make the Rooster's Regret, a fly with four brown feathers tied to a hook. So the Ball's Camp flies with white feathers may be among the earliest references in Maine to what we know today as the streamer fly. I have talked to many people about the subject. No one can confirm my theory. Nor can anyone refute it.

Carrie Stevens was a milliner who made feather adornments for men's and women's hats. A common embellishment for a gentleman's hat of the time consisted of two or three feathers cemented together. The application of this decoration to the right and left side of a hook made a compound or complex wing with a cheek. Adding some bucktail on the under-

body for stability, to keep the fly from rolling over, was probably a natural step for her to take. On July 1, 1924, Stevens fished this fly, the Gray Ghost, in Upper Dam Pool and caught a nearly seven-pound brook trout. Her husband Wallace was a guide, and Carrie began receiving orders to make the fly. Shortly thereafter, she was tying streamer flies with many different feathers. Joseph Bates showed me examples of Stevens's flies that he had included in his 1950 book, *Fly Fishing in Fresh and Salt Water.* Some of her early flies made with feathers and bucktail were very crude and didn't even have names, but she went on to originate a number of patterns and to tie flies for many famous and wealthy sportsmen who went to the Rangeley Lakes area.

Although I can tie just about any kind of streamer, I prefer the style of streamer with the complex feather wing that veils the hook on either side. The streamers I tie are intended to be fished for the true landlocked salmon, not for black salmon or winter-over salmon in rivers. Many tyers are unwilling to spend the time needed to tie these flies. Their simple appearance is deceptive, and there are no shortcuts. What takes time is learning the properties of the materials and selecting materials that are going to give me the results I want. In the years since I first began tying, I have refined, added to, and slightly

modified some of the aspects of Stevens's assembly. Austin Hogan's dressings were influential as well, especially his blendings of color in the feather wings. I slightly altered the positioning of the wings and contributed my own sense of color and design. The experience of studying art gave me a trained eye for compositional balance and color harmony. Art is essentially a honed way of seeing, which I have been able to bring to my flytying.

I have an idea in my mind of what a perfect fly is, and I probably achieve it one time in ten. I guess that is the challenge of being an artist or craftsman. An artist can always find something wrong with a painting. A musician is rarely satisfied with a record. I can always find a flaw in a fly. In spite of this, I enjoy imagining a fly in my mind and attempting to create it. There are no new rock-and-roll songs, but it is possible to come up with something a little different that sounds good. The same is true of the streamer medium. There are combinations of colors and feathers that I have yet to try, and this vast potential keeps me going. I feel satisfaction in knowing that the heritage of a streamer I tie lies in a classic form of flytying in the Northeast. However gorgeous a fly is, it can be tied to some six-pound-test leader and put out well behind a boat on a brutal, rainy landlocked salmon afternoon in April or May, and catch a fish.

BOB VEVERKA

When I was growing up in Long Island, New York, no one I knew fly-fished or tied flies. From the age of six, I fished with spinning gear for trout, bass, and even more often for saltwater fish like weakfish, bluefish, and striped bass. My aunt, who knew how much I enjoyed fishing, once took me to William Mills & Son in New York City to look at all the equipment and buy me a couple of spinning lures. Only later did I realize that William Mills was such a fly-fishing mecca on the east coast. Through books, I became interested in fly-fishing and bought myself a fly rod. The first fish I caught was a bass—and that was the beginning.

As a teenager, I became friends with a schoolmate whose father, Fred West, fished for trout and tied flies. I never got a chance to tie flies with him, but he was the one who gave me the idea of making my own fishing flies. For ten dollars, I bought a little flytying kit with a rickety old vise and a few feathers. My first flies were very crude, simple trout flies, bucktails, and streamers. I started to look at the pictures of flies in the Orvis catalogs and wanted to have one of everything. I was unable to afford to buy so many flies all at once, but gradually accumulated a box full of Orvis flies. I had the box with me one day when I was fishing, and lost it. I was so heartbroken that I gave up fly-fishing for five years.

What changed my mind was stopping at an Orvis store in eastern Long Island while I was on one of my saltwater fishing trips.

LEFT: *Three-Eyed Monster* I had looked at the flies on display and was on my way out the door when the salesman told me that the flies were on sale for half price. I bought a couple dozen flies and was back into fly-fishing again. I started to fish on the Connequot River on Long Island, where I caught a lot of trout. The river used to be owned by the Southside Sportsman's Club and then the state took it over and opened it for fishing. The water was clear and filled with big trout. Because I could watch the fish, I learned about the habits of the trout and how they fed. I could see them rise to my fly. As I branched out, I started to fish in Pennsylvania and in upstate New York on the Beaverkill River and many of the lakes. All of the flies I tied were for my fishing—dry flies, nymphs, streamers, bucktails, big, buggy-looking flies.

After I moved to Vermont in 1980, I turned to landlocked salmon flies such as the Carrie Stevens streamers that were so popular in New England. Streamer flies, with their long, sleek shape and hackles of different colors, have a style all their own. I started to feel that, to be a good flytyer, I should be able to tie the whole range of flies, and that is what I sought to do, by proceeding in stages. Using Trey Combs's book *Steelhead Fly Fishing and Flies*, I began to tie steelhead flies and Spey flies. Then I wondered what was left. So I moved on to Atlantic salmon flies, first hair-wings, then full-dress feather-wing flies. I found Atlantic salmon flies fascinating to look at but knew very little about the techniques and materials needed to tie them. I thought that I could never tie something so difficult and complex as an Atlantic salmon fly.

In the late 1970s, more people were tying Atlantic salmon flies than had been tying them before. Among them was Bill Hunter, who helped me get started. Bill was and still is one of the top Atlantic salmon fly tyers in the country. When I saw his flies in the Hunter's Angling catalog, I knew that they had a special style and decided to take a class from him at his shop in New Boston, New Hampshire. Bill taught how to use hooks and materials, think about proportions, and make a neat fly with a smooth tag and body, a properly set tail, precisely married feathers, and well-positioned wings. The first book I bought on Atlantic salmon flies, as did many tyers, was Poul

Jorgensen's *Salmon Flies*, which helped me with patterns and techniques. His book was very influential then because it was *the* book on the subject and covered a wide range of flies. From my reading, I gradually learned about the history of the flies I was tying. For the history, especially of specific patterns and their originators, Joseph Bates's books are the best. Contemporary authors write about flies as if everything is a new invention, but Joe knew the importance of history.

When I decided to tie flies commercially, I ran an ad in a local Vermont sports paper. I specialized in streamers for individual customers, and for a year, before my own business became too demanding, I tied streamers for Hunter's Angling Supplies. With the abundant lake fishing in the Northeast, the demand for streamers was high but few tyers were making them. Even now, good streamer tyers are rarer than Atlantic salmon fly tyers. At first I tied three or four patterns for Hunter's, including the Gray Ghost, the Counterfeiter, and the Maynard's Marvel, which required twenty-four golden pheasant crests. The list grew to twenty different patterns. I appreciated tying for Bill because he felt that American tyers were skilled and wanted to support them instead of selling imported flies. It was a hard decision to stop tying for him, but since then I have never been without business.

Many customers ask me to tie Spey flies for steelhead fishing on the west coast. Someone may wonder what a tyer living in Vermont knows about a traditional Scottish fly and fishing it for steelhead. I have always liked tying Spey flies, and they are some of the finest flies I tie. I remember the first Spey fly I saw. On a trip to fish the Beaverkill River in upstate New York, I went into Elsie and Harry Darbee's shop in Roscoe. Among all the materials and other items displayed on one wall was a group of five framed flies. The one that caught my eye was a fly with very long, graceful hackles. "You like that?" Harry said. "That's a Spey fly." He told me it was by Charles DeFeo and that it was very hard to tie. The next Spey I saw was by Syd Glasso, who became the major source of inspiration for my tying.

I first learned of Glasso in Trey Combs's book, which included a plate of his Spey flies. I was struck by his Speys because of their sleek lines, flowing hackles, long-shank hooks, and small heads, and by his artistic eye for combining colors and materials. I could see that Glasso knew what he was doing and that no one else was tying the way he was. Bill Hunter knew Glasso, and when I took the flytying course from

Bill, he showed me pictures of Glasso's full-dress flies. I couldn't believe how beautiful they were. "So here's the same guy," I thought, "who is in Combs's book." I asked Bill for Glasso's address, and Bill told me to wait before I wrote him because he was very ill. About six months later, after I had tied some Spey flies, I thought that I would write Glasso. I asked Bill again for his address, but he told me that Glasso had just died. It was as if a part of me had just been lost. He was the most significant person to inspire me—and I never knew him.

After Glasso's death, it was hard to find out about his tying, so I started to seek out people who had known him. Glasso never sold any of his flies, and locating original examples was difficult. Each person I contacted would share a bit of information with me or show me some Spey flies he had tied. Finally, I just had to sit down and attempt to determine how he made his Speys. What really set the style of Glasso's flies was the hooks he used. They had long shanks, which caused the wing to sit low along the hook. I tried to create a similarly graceful fly with a neat little head so that the fly seems to expand from the head. It took many hours to achieve what I wanted, and I cut many flies off the hook.

I have fished Spey flies for steelhead in the Northwest and for Atlantic salmon in eastern Canada. The technique I use is to quarter the fly downstream and allow it to sweep through the water. As the fly drops back and stops, I move my wrist a little so that the hackles on the fly pulsate. The hackles act like legs and entice the fish. It is this movement that will trigger an Atlantic salmon or steelhead to strike, whether the response is aggression or the memory of food when the fish was younger. Many of my trout flies are similar to Spey flies, with hackles that move in the water. These are qualities I think about when I build my flies.

In addition to tying traditional salmon flies, I create my own patterns. I start with a certain feather—a hackle or a feather for a wing—on which I will base the fly. There are always a couple of feathers that are different from all the others. Around that unique feather, I will build a pattern. When I make my own patterns, I can leave out parts that I don't like to tie or am less confident about. I find that the first time I tie a fly—whether a known pattern or a pattern of my own—it comes out the best. If I try to do it again, it is impossible to match the first fly. That is why I keep that first fly. I don't know if my eye picks out the best feathers to use, or if I am more

ABOVE:

Tri-Color Spey

relaxed when tying a fly for the first time.

The foundation of all my flies is the hook, and I dress a fly according to the hook's form and proportions. It's as if the fly is custom-made for the hook. If I tied five different Jock Scotts on five different hooks, they would all be different. Other tyers might make all the flies the same, but because my dressing of the fly is based on the hook I have chosen, certain elements in each Jock Scott will be distinctive in order that the fly be symmetrical and in proportion to the hook. I use all kinds of hooks—various antiques, contemporary hooks by Eugene Sunday. I prefer to tie with a long-shank hook because I want to make a fly that flows with the hook, as if it were under water, even though it is still in the vise. Occa-

sionally I have had a good hook that I can no longer obtain, and some of the nicest flies I have tied have been on those hooks. Since I will never find the hooks again, I will never tie the flies the same way.

I like to tie flies as much as I like to fish, maybe more, and I don't fish as often now as I used to. I can relax and enjoy myself just as much right here, at my vise. I am drawn to natural materials, to the furs and feathers and their textures and colors. When I tie flies, my mind is many miles away. Most of the time, I am thinking about fishing. I remember my experiences and try to incorporate what I learn on the stream into my flies. Whether I am fishing or tying, I know that there is nothing as beautiful as nature.

CHARLIE KROM

YULAN, NEW YORK

I think of myself as a versatile tyer. Hair-wing salmon flies, wet flies and dry flies for trout, realistic nymphs, salt-water flies—I get pleasure from tying all of them. But the first type of fly I fell in love with when I started tying in the early 1950s was wet flies, primarily because I was attracted to the color. My mother happened to bring home a copy of *Family Circle* magazine. When I browsed through it, I saw an article on flytying. It struck me like a kick in the head. The wet flies were the ones that grabbed my attention. There were several pages of them, the Silver Doctor, Parmachene Belle, Wickham's Fancy. Little did I know then that I would become so involved in flytying and fly-fishing.

Eventually I tied so many wet flies that I had to do something with them. The Angler's Cove in midtown Manhattan was the shop I went to most frequently. The Cove was a very prestigious store, on a par with Abercrombie and Fitch. It was well stocked and had beautiful displays in the storefront. I approached the owner, Andy Lipman, and showed him my wet flies, and he began selling them in the store. Before Andy sold the shop in 1960, I also helped him by repairing reels and other tackle. After the store was sold, I worked at the counter intermittently for eight years during my time off from the fire department. I continued to tie wet flies for the shop and grew to love commercial tying so much that I could tie flies all day and into the night.

The Angler's Cove was a center for people interested in fly-fishing. You pick a name in the fly-fishing world and I met that person. Trout fishing was becoming increasingly popular in the 1960s, and there was a big demand for trout flies. It was not uncommon for someone to come into the store and buy a couple hundred dollars' worth of trout flies. I knew very few people who tied Atlantic salmon flies or went fishing for salmon. The salmon flies at the store were around for years because no one bought them. Lee Wulff had some of his plastic flies in the store and they remained there until the Cove was sold.

Lee Wulff was one of the few people I knew back then who did fish for salmon. Lee had a big impact on salmon fishing through his writing and his flies. He was an innovator in his tying, always experimenting. He came into the store a few times. He always liked to talk about salmon fishing and would think nothing about tying a fly while he was there. He was not someone who had secrets. One day he sat down at the table and tied a fly he called the Prefontaine, which consisted of two saddle hackles and bucktail, tied on a size 20 hook, holding the hook in his fingers, not in a vise. One, two, three—and he was finished.

Keith Fulsher was another person I met at the Angler's Cove because he also tied flies for the store. He had already fished for Atlantic salmon when I went with him to the Miramichi River in New Brunswick on my first salmon-fishing trip. On that initial trip we took together, we fished at Gray Rapids on the Miramichi. I was using a fly called the Brown Mystery—and hooked a salmon. I never saw the fish but when it took the line I was hooked for life. A salmon never takes a fly the way a trout does. It's not a hit but a pull. The line gets taut, and line, leader, and rod are strained to their limit. At that point, you better set the drag on the reel and brace yourself for that initial run and the sound of the screaming reel. That's what hooking a salmon is all about.

After that trip, Keith and I went to New Brunswick every year. Jack Story was often our guide. He lived in Storytown, across the Miramichi from Doaktown. Our favorite pool was right in Doaktown, where the Miramichi Salmon Museum is now located. It was beautiful water. Right where the utility wires went across the river was the cabin where Frank Bondatti, for whom the Bondatti Killer was named, had his camp.

ABOVE, CLOCKWISE FROM TOP:

Silver Monkey

Blue Doctor

Gold Fever

Helmsdale Doctor

Copper Killer

The same road to Bondatti's cabin went past Jack's house. Keith and I stayed at Bondatti's cabin for several seasons. Every morning, just before the sun came up, we would catch our limit—on a Fulkro Special. That's where Keith and I developed the fly, and we always had good results with it.

Jack didn't tie flies but loved to fish. He was a dedicated guide. He never complained when Keith and I spent fourteen hours a day fishing. I would say to Jack, "We'd like to go out tomorrow, right at dawn." The next morning, we would be in the cabin getting ready to leave at five, and at four-thirty Jack would be sitting on the veranda of the cabin, waiting to go down to the river. He never went home to eat. He would rather stay on the river. Keith and I would go up to the cabin for lunch. Afterward, when we went back down to the river, he would be playing a fish, ready to hand it over to one of us to bring in. Jack liked to go through anyone's fly box. If you pointed to a fly and asked him what he thought of it, he would say enthusiastically, "Oh that's it. That's the fly." Whichever fly you showed him, it was the one to use. He would be overjoyed if you gave him a few flies.

As Keith and I did more fishing and tying, we started to research Atlantic salmon hair-wing flies. As best we could, we investigated the history of the hair-wing. To our knowledge, one of the earliest fishing flies was the Red Devon, made from the hair of a red Devon cow. It dates from the early days when northeastern Canada was first settled. The local people had no way to get the materials for feather-wing salmon flies, so they used what was available. Where were they going to get the swan and European jay used in the more traditional patterns? When Keith and I were working on our book, *Hair-Wing Atlantic Salmon Flies*, we were going to try to name the flies after the people who invented or designed them. But we realized there are so many versions of the same patterns that it would be impossible to identify the originators with any accuracy.

Charlie DeFeo shared a lot of patterns and tying ideas with me. He lived in Manhattan and came in the Angler's Cove two or three times a week, often on his lunch hour. It was always a pleasure to see him. Whereas many people only talked the salmon-fishing game, Charlie knew the game. I often watched Charlie tie. No matter what subject you started talking about—baseball or taxes—the conversation always wound up about salmon. Charlie contributed a lot to tying salmon flies and fishing for salmon. He was really the one who started to popularize colorful hair-wing patterns. Many of the hair-wings and the reduced feather-wings of the time, such as Ira Gruber's, were very somber. Since Charlie was an artist by profession, he liked to try out different color combinations. Because he tied so many flies, there are thousands of them out there in the field and in private collections.

Charlie was very kind and generous. When I told Charlie I was going fishing, he would say, "I have some patterns for you." Keith and I were headed for New Brunswick one day, and I saw Charlie right before we left. "If I knew you were going," he said, "I would have given you some flies." Charlie mailed the flies to the motel in Doaktown where Keith and I were staying. I still have the envelope they came in. One of the flies was a small iridescent fly that Charlie called a Bird of Paradise. I never fished with it because I never had a fly with a bird of paradise feather.

What was special about Charlie was that he was so innovative. He always used to say, "The day I think I know it all is the day it's over with." I feel the same way. I like challenges. I guess I could say that Charlie and I were on a similar course. Like Charlie, I prefer sparsely tied flies. Over the years I have come to appreciate the slimness of a fly. An Atlantic salmon fly doesn't have to be a big, gaudy attractor. All it needs to be effective are a few pieces of hair and a little tinsel. I like using the least amount of materials to get the same results. I also enjoy experimenting with new materials, particularly man-made materials. I don't want a fly to look like a spinning lure. Certain synthetic or man-made materials are inappropriate for feather-wing flies, but they are suitable for hair-wings. I once used tinsel for the bodies of my flies, but because it tarnishes, I now use Mylar piping on patterns where it can be substituted for tinsel and ribbing. Mylar also takes dyes very well, particularly copper, and makes an excellent Copper Killer, a tremendously effective salmon fly.

Rather than making the wing of a fly from hair alone, I tie in fibers of floss under the hair. I take a piece of floss, hold it with one hand, and pull it sharply with the fingertips of the other hand. The floss unravels and the fibers separate and flare out. The light catches the floss in the wing, making for a glittering iridescence that attracts the salmon. The Silver Monkey is a DeFeo pattern with floss in the wing. I have changed the pattern slightly by adding a fluorescent red tip and a Mylar piping body.

When you tie and fish a lot, you naturally want to try something different. Before you experiment, though, it is important to learn the basics. There should be no rules for designing flies and no limit on the materials you can use, but tying procedures need to have standards. Anybody can put materials on a hook, and an unattractive, poorly tied fly can catch as many salmon as a beautiful, meticulously tied fly. For my own personal satisfaction, I want to refine a fly. I spend a lot of time being fussy. When I go back to look at a fly a few months after I have tied it, I may not think it is still beautiful, yet I always learn something from it. I will never reach a point where my tying ability will level off. With every fly, I seem to be getting better at something. Once you have the ability, you never lose it. It is all here, stored in these hands.

PAUL SCHMOOKLER

MILLIS, MASSACHUSETTS

My attraction to the magic of Atlantic salmon flies began with an innocent first look. In the late 1960s, I met a man fishing the Muscoot River, better known as the Amawalk Outlet, in Westchester County, New York. This gentleman was visiting the United States from Spain and, like all fly-fishermen, took great pride in his flies. Although we were fishing for trout, the subject turned to salmon flies, and before long he showed me three black japanned boxes filled with salmon flies, which he had in the back of his car. When I looked at these flies, I saw an array of colors and shapes like nothing I had seen before. To the eyes of a novice, they were like beautiful gems. The flies, I later found out, had been tied by Belarmino Martinez, in my opinion one of the finest commercial salmon fly tyers in the world.

Even before I started to tie Atlantic salmon flies, I collected materials. In the 1960s, I was authorized to collect biological specimens for numerous supply houses, museums, and universities. This allowed me to travel across the globe and become well known as a professional field collector. It was natural that my love of entomology and ornithology would continue into my hobbies and my art. Through collecting butterflies, I became friends with an elderly gentleman who, at the time, owned one of the largest butterfly supply houses in the world. In 1968, I bought a portion of this gentleman's business, became a distributor of glass domes for display, and in the domes made creative arrangements of butterflies on artificial flowers. A year later, I started to make compositions in

ABOVE:

Comet

the domes using artistically tied artificial mayflies, caddisflies, and stoneflies.

Around 1970, this same gentleman I had befriended through collecting butterflies pulled me aside and showed me a crate filled with bird specimens from the 1930s. They had been sent to him by various other butterfly suppliers as a ploy to see if he was interested in selling them. Until that time, nobody had shown any interest in this collection, and he had advised his suppliers not to send any further specimens. When I saw the collection of skins, I knew I had to have them — for what I had no idea—but as a collector, I just had to have them. By that time I had already been tying trout flies for ten years and was ready to experiment with something new. It wasn't long before I realized that these feathers gave me the potential to be as fanciful and as experimental with my tying as I wished.

Ever since I can remember, I have always been what some might call a "frustrated artist." No matter how hard I tried, I knew I would never be a painter, but I still felt that I could express my artistic abilities through creative flytying. To that end, I have always viewed feathers as my paints and the hook as my canvas. Only a handful of American tyers in the 1960s were interested in salmon flies, and they were tying only popular classic patterns. Not wanting to be like all the rest, I chose to pioneer and inspire artistic and creative salmon fly tying by developing unusual patterns other than those published in the past literature. By the mid-1970s, the more I tied, the better I became—and the better I became, the more I enjoyed it. The success of being able to meet any challenge in flytying, and meet it in my own way and on my own terms, drove me on.

After over twelve years of tying both classic and artistic Atlantic salmon flies, I grew able to envision a completed fly in my head. Just like a professional chess player who sees a hundred moves before a game starts, I can see a salmon fly in its totality a month or more before I tie it. When I have an idea for a fly, the pattern simply flows forth, and I don't have to guess what types of material I will need later when I sit down to tie it. When the creative spirit hits me, sometimes I will get up at two or three in the morning to make notes about the fly. At other times the image of the fly will be ingrained so strongly in my mind that notes are unnecessary. When it comes to salmon flies, my mind is like a file cabinet, and I can go into the files and find images whenever I need them. Before I ever sit down to tie, I form a mental image of all the necessary materials. I have memorized my extensive inventory of materials and know the shape, characteristics, and capabilities of every feather. When I think of a fly pattern, I can picture where every component is located in the collection—it's like going to a library and being able to take out any book I want.

Whether someone is tying classic salmon flies or artistic salmon flies, I believe that form and composition are very important. Each fly is composed of different elements that complement one another. I prefer to avoid harsh lines and therefore use many circular, elliptical, and spherical shapes. When I tie a fly, I seek to create a flow—a calm wave of color. There are tricks in the art field that can benefit the flytyer. My "new generation" married-wing flies, which I first tied in 1987, incorporate single strips of black. I enjoy watching television shows about painting. On one program, an artist was talking about highlighting and shadowing. What better way to bring out a lighter color than by highlighting it with a darker color? So I started marrying single or double strips of black fibers in between each brightly colored strip in the wing in order to bring out, or contrast, the lighter colors. The effect was staggering.

For inspiration on color combinations, I often visit museums, art stores, and tropical aquariums. I am less interested in color for the sake of color than in colors that are recognizable, if only by suggestion. In my artistic flies, I use

OPPOSITE:

Double Leopard

concepts of color and symmetry related to the insects and animals that I enjoy observing and photographing. People looking at one of the flies may feel they have seen the colors or the form before, but they cannot pinpoint where. I also choose colors for their emotional expressiveness and their subliminal qualities. Many tyers are unaware of the psychological qualities of color.

In 1986, I created a particular fly called the Bird of Paradise. It is not based on any bird but rather on the Hawaiian flower of the same name that can be seen in almost any supermarket flower shop. The flower grows at a right angle to the stem and resembles the wing of a salmon fly. If you look at the flower carefully, you can almost see feathered, married-wing strips. I decided to capture the combination of green, orange, and red of the paradise flower in a salmon fly. When people saw the fly, they did not see what I saw, but they found it haunting—and kept trying to remember where they had seen that color combination before. The fly was a success.

Authentic salmon fly tying material—it drives some individuals to their limits trying to acquire it. I have always been the consummate collector of material, having started at a time when supplies were available and nobody was remotely interested in them. Today, there are some tyers who, like piranhas, go into a buying frenzy whenever they find anything that can be used in salmon flies. For the most part, new tyers are having a hard time finding particular materials and have had to look for substitutes. I have created a series of substitutes for Indian crow, toucan, and blue chatterer, which I thought would be useful for tyers. These feathers are just as good as the authentic materials and just as easy, if not easier, to use because of their feather structure. I continue to tie with the material from my collection, but if the day comes when I must use substitutes or synthetics, I will use them.

I strongly believe that if George Kelsen, William Blacker, James Rogan, and other tyers of the past had been able to obtain synthetics, they all would have tied with them. For the nineteenth century tyers, their natural materials were like the Flashabou and Krystal Flash of today. Furthermore, it was these tyers who came up with the theory that using reflective and refractive materials in flies would attract game fish. They were the ones responsible for incorporating iridescent materials in

Atlantic salmon flies. Many people have theorized that the tyers of the nineteenth century were competing with each other to come up with better ideas and materials. But that, I believe, is a modern viewpoint based on competitive tying in the late twentieth century. In the last century and until the 1960s, tyers of salmon flies had no choice but to explore the principles of reflection and refraction using natural materials that embodied these qualities, because they were the only ones available.

Students of flytying literature often wonder where the eighteenth and nineteenth century salmon fly tyers obtained their materials, which must have been rare since such materials were not sold in sport shops. Here, again, the twentieth century mentality is unable to take into account how easy it was at the turn of the century, and even earlier, to obtain these items. One such place in particular, Steven's Auction House, a biological supply and auction house in Covent Garden in London, was active from the late 1780s through the 1890s and sold rare and exotic bird and butterfly specimens every day of the week, largely to collectors and armchair scientists. European explorers sweating it out in Central and South America, Africa, and the East Indies were sending their finds back to England, where scholars and collectors were identifying and labeling them.

In the process of my research, I estimate that about seven hundred fifty Indian crow specimens arrived in England during the last half of the nineteenth century, and I believe we are still using feathers from ninety percent of those original birds. Although additional birds have been collected since, I know that more people have walked on the face of the moon than have seen an Indian crow in the wild. No more than four or five human beings, myself included, have spotted Indian crow in its natural habitat. One of the first feathers that your eye is drawn to in an Atlantic salmon fly is from the Indian crow. *Pyroderus scutatus*—it's a great name, *pyroderus* meaning "fire skin" and *scutatus* meaning "armed with a shield." It's a very fanciful name for a bird with a shield-shaped breast that is a brilliant, shimmering fiery red.

When I think about the past, I am attracted to two periods of history. I always wanted to belong to the generation before me—the era of Charlie DeFeo, Preston Jennings, and the Canadian tyers of the 1940s who experimented with prismatic flies. I also look back to the late 1880s to Major John P. Traherne. I admire his flies because, coincidentally, I started tying in his style before I knew anything about him. He created such patterns as the Chatterer, Jay PT, and Nellie Bly—the same types of flies with the whole wings and multiple golden pheasant crests that I enjoy doing today. Traherne tied flies for fishing just about as much as he did for show, but he also talked about how tying salmon flies could provide a challenge for the flytyer.

And here is the belief that I live by: The past with its classic flies is just that—the past, and someone else's work. Flytyers should experiment and create artistic flies from their imagination and in that way progress into the future. There is a considerable difference between the artist and the craftsman. The artist works from the imagination, while the craftsman works from a set of instructions, usually someone else's. This is not to say that a craftsman cannot be a master, but I believe the greater satisfaction is attained from originality.

BILL HUNTER

NEW BOSTON, NEW HAMPSHIRE

When I started tying Atlantic salmon flies, I tied them to fish. On my first trip to the Restigouche River in New Brunswick, I took a 1/0 Jock Scott and was delighted to hook a forty-one-pound salmon on the third day of the trip. I went on to hook seven thirty-pound-plus fish that week on full-dress flies. Although I have been unable to duplicate the experience, that trip gave me great impetus to return home and continue tying salmon flies. My basic reason for tying is still as a means to catch fish more than as a demonstration of art, and I still prefer feather-wing flies. They fish well, they catch as many or more fish than hair-wings, and they are attractive.

The flies I use are traditional patterns—Green Highlanders, Jock Scotts, Dusty Millers, Black Doses—but I modify the flies by slimming them down so that they are faster and easier to tie, yet are just as effective. Rather than spend my whole day at the flytying bench, I want to be out on the river. I need to tie a Jock Scott in fifteen minutes, not in an hour and a half, so I alter my choice of materials and tying tactics. Not only do I want to make a fly quickly, but I avoid using materials that will result in a fly that costs forty dollars to tie. Tying Atlantic salmon flies is perceived as being very difficult. It is really an application of the same basic skills used to make trout flies. Since you are tying more materials on the hook, you have to think about each step before you do it.

The Restigouche, which remains my favorite river for Atlantic salmon, is a beautiful, classic salmon river filled with large fish. The conditions change throughout the season. During the first two weeks of June, when the water is high, a big fly is needed to get the attention of the fish. For the rest of the season, when the water is down, the fish will hit size 6s down to 10s and 12s. When tyers make a fly to frame, they make it large so people can see it. Most of my flies are small because they are

tied for fishing. I believe it was Syd Glasso who had one of the greatest observations on the scale of flies: "Some tyers are like rock bands. If they can't make good music, they make louder music." Syd never tied flies bigger than a size 1.

I have invented a couple of patterns for Atlantic salmon but they did not offer more than the existing stock of patterns. With thousands of patterns available, it is hard to create a new one. Part of the satisfaction of a fishing trip, however, is experimenting with the selection of flies. In Atlantic salmon fishing, there is no consistency—or little justifiable consistency—and the chances are just as good as not that any fly will work. Salmon are not feeding, and because they will hit almost anything, I can readily choose what I want to fish with. That attitude rarely works in trout fishing. One of the reasons that Atlantic salmon flies catch fish is not what the fish think but is what *we* think. A fly is not more effective because it attracts fish, so much as it is effective because it attracts the fisherman, who tends to fish the pattern with more conviction, thus more concentration and more persistence, and ultimately more hook-ups.

If you fish for Atlantic salmon, you tend to ask more questions of your flies from the standpoint of practicality. I wonder, Can I make these flies faster? Can I make them more soundly? Yet if you never fish the Atlantic salmon flies that you tie, you can still tie a good fly. Many tyers who have never fished for salmon produce beautiful flies—at least to hang on the wall—and I can appreciate this purely artistic approach to tying. In this sense, there are two different schools or approaches, each of which produces two distinct-looking flies. If you put them side by side, you can see that, while they have similarities, they have just as many differences. Flytying is an opportunity to play god every day. When tyers sit down at the vise, they are "in charge" and can be just as creative or artistic

ABOVE, FROM TOP:

Green Highlander
Black Doctor

as they want to be. They determine the color of a fly, how big or how little, intricate or simple, it will be. Not only do they make all these decisions, but they can complete the fly in twenty minutes if they want. This potential fits the American psyche well in that there is an instant product.

The late Syd Glasso was the tyer I admired the most and the one who made the greatest impression on me. Syd had a way of creating form and symmetry that were extremely pleasing to the eye. I am not sure how he achieved what he did, even though I know what feathers he used. I met Syd in Seattle at a sports show in the mid-1970s and had an opportunity to talk with him every day of the show. Some of the things Syd did were very clever. Not only was he an excellent tyer but he was a thinker. He realized that the hook often dictated the final form of the fly, so he started to make his own hooks in order to achieve the particular symmetry he wanted.

And he figured out how to do it cheaply. What I learned from Syd was to ask questions. Throughout the week of the show, Syd asked me a lot of questions, which made me ask still more questions and look for even more answers, and try harder at what I was doing in my tying.

I also admired Poul Jorgensen because he organized so much information on Atlantic salmon flies and ultimately wrote it down in a book. He was active early in the emerging interest in salmon flies twenty years ago, and he was able to present the material in a very readable form. After my wife Simone and I opened Hunter's Angling Supplies in our house in 1973, Poul would visit us in New Boston, and I started to watch him tie flies and learn from him. Just after his book *Salmon Flies* came out in 1978, Poul taught his first class at our shop when it was still at the house. The ten people taking the class sat around the table in our dining room. Outside the big window at the end of the room were eight or ten guys who had not paid for the class but were standing on the flower beds looking in the window to see what Poul was doing. That a class on tying Atlantic salmon flies would be this compelling made a big impact on me. I still have a large photograph showing all the rubberneckers peering in the window.

Hunter's Angling Supplies was often associated with the Atlantic salmon fly because it was one of the few shops offering classes in the 1970s. People flew in from around the country to attend my early salmon fly classes. From occupying one or two rooms, the business grew to take over the entire house. In 1979, a location in town became available, so we took it. The move got the customers out of the house. People had been in the house all hours of the day and night, and the phone was constantly ringing. The shop was financially successful for twelve of the fifteen years we were in business, and when we sold it in 1988, we were ready to move on. It was a great experience and I would do it again.

In the beginning, we were sort of "zoned" into opening the business. One day in October of 1973, two of the selectmen in town, who happened to be fly-fishers, came over to the house and mentioned that there was going to be a vote on restrictive zoning for the residential area of New Boston. If you ever want to open a shop, they said, do it tonight because the vote is tomorrow. We put eighteen dollars in a bank account, and painted a sign and hung it up at about ten o'clock at night. I gathered up all my flies and put them in a plastic box on the bureau. We had a bank account, a sign, and merchandise. The next day the zoning was passed.

After Hunter's Angling opened, I was spending quite a few hours a day at the vise tying commercially for the shop and for individual clients. I was using a rotary tying vise, which was common then but did not hold up to commercial tying. Someone suggested that I consider designing my own vise. Intrigued by this idea, I started doodling on paper. The next thing I knew, I was getting more and more involved, hiring machinists, making prototypes, and asking tyers to try them out. When I had refined the designs, I approached a gun manufacturer, Thompson Center Arms, which put its casting lab at my disposal so I could test a method for making the necessary parts. After learning about machining, investment casting, and metallurgy, I finalized the design. Some unique casting techniques were developed in the process. We set up equipment in the basement of the house and actually did secondary machining as well as fitting and assembly.

When I went to Sun Valley, Idaho, for the 1976 national conclave of the Federation of Fly Fishers, I showed one of the vises to Bonnie and René Harrop. Fascinated with it, they asked why I had chosen to make it the way I did. I said, "Because it will last forever." René reached under the table and pulled out a cardboard box that contained forty-odd broken vises. René and Bonnie were intense tyers, and they bought vises by the dozen, knowing that one would give out every couple of weeks. This shoddy quality is what prompted me to make the HMH vise. When the vise was released that year, people told me it would be crazy to spend so much money on a flytying vise. The most expensive ones available at the time cost about twenty dollars. The first HMH vises were priced at over eighty dollars. I told tyers that the vises not only worked better than most others on the market but would last forever —and today those early vises sell for eight hundred to eleven hundred dollars. If HMH is remembered for anything, it will be that it opened the door for many other well-made vises in the late 1970s. It also hit at the right time. Fly-fishing and fly-tying were starting to grow in popularity and American tyers were willing to pay for a reliable product.

The name for the vise came from a German engraver. When we were setting up the vise business and preparing for the Idaho conclave, our lawyer told us that we needed a product name to ensure patent protection. I had never given the name a thought. Since I was leaving the next day, I called up Fred and asked him to engrave New Boston Vise Co. on the parts, for lack of a better name. The atmosphere at the house where we first had the shop was always zany, and every time the engraver showed up, it was full of fishermen and laughter. So when he called back five or six hours later, I had a hard time understanding him because some rowdies were talking noisily in the background and Fred had a thick German accent. He was trying to tell me that he was unable to fit the name on the vise part. I just said, "Put Hunter on it. Put anything on it. I need a name on there by tomorrow." He showed up a while later, with the parts marked "HMH." Fly-fishing had never made much sense to him, and when I asked him what it meant, he said, "Zee place is full of veerdoes. It's a mad house. It's Hunter's Mad House. You don't like it—tough." He left the shop and I left the name on.

As the primary teacher at the shop, I taught classes in hair-wing and feather-wing salmon flies, and as many classes in trout flies. I always believed in hands-on teaching, not in demonstrating, and liked to spend time with every person in the class, looking over his or her shoulder. I enjoy seeing people learn to do something that they did not believe they could do. It was the same when I taught a junior ski-racing program. It was an infectious undertaking and had to be one of the most compulsive pursuits I was ever involved in. As the kids looked down the gates on the slope for the first time, they had little confidence that they could ever ski through all those bamboo poles. Not only could they ski through them after two or three tries, but they could do it quickly—and without noticing that I kept tightening the gates. Flytying is equally satisfying. Seeing people accomplish something they didn't think they could gives me a good feeling and gives them a great feeling. Some of the people I had the pleasure of teaching flytying to included such talents as Bob Veverka, Wayne Luallen, Jim Taylor, Dick Talleur, Charles Chute, Bob Warren, Jack Gartside, and Warren Duncan.

Teaching flytying began unexpectedly for me. In 1966, a year after Simone and I were married, I was working at a sporting goods store. The owner asked the old-timer who tied commercially for the store to teach a flytying class and wanted me to take the class so I could also tie flies for the shop. The old-timer came in and taught the first class, then had a heart attack and became incapacitated. Here we had eight or nine people who had paid for the class and now were without an instructor. Since the shop never gave refunds, I wondered how the owner was going to get out of this situation. His solution was to turn to me and say, "Bill, you teach the class." So I had taken only one class and was going to teach the remaining sessions. After some arguing back and forth, I decided to go home, read some books, and quickly learn to tie. What I was learning on Tuesday, I was teaching on Thursday. I did not make any pretenses of being a pro but somehow it worked. That was my first class—my first class was my first class.

After the class was over, I started tying on my own, for myself and a handful of customers. There were few professional tyers in those days. Later I met Charlie Beausoleil, another commercial tyer, who sold flies to Orvis and other shops. Everything about tying, according to Charlie, was very mysterious. It was magic, as if done with mirrors. Charlie had a room in his basement filled with stuff. He would pull down the shades, check outside the door, shut the door, and swear me to secrecy. Then all he did was show me how to tie the wing on a wet fly. Two days later, I could read the same information in *Field and Stream*, but for Charlie it was a big secret. Many other tyers of the time were reluctant to share information with a tyer who was in competition with them. I have often thought that this attitude was a throwback to the days of the ghillies, who were very competitive and were some of the world's foremost con men.

Later, when I taught classes at my own shop, I realized that teaching flytying, especially Atlantic salmon flies, was a kind of trap. In between teaching the classes, I had to find materials. I read through some of the old books, which used terms that were out of date or confusing. After sorting out this information, I established what was usable material and what was not. I went into suppliers' back rooms and discovered materials they didn't even know were valuable. A feather merchant would have a price list that said goose *coquilles*. What is that? I looked in George Kelson's 1895 *The Salmon Fly*, which called for goose *nageoires*. Then I went to J. Edson Leonard's 1950 *Flies*, which said, in effect, "Get some goose shoulders." By a process of elimination, I figured out what I really needed. I would also find old flies and compare the materials on them with those sold by the feather merchants. Since then, books by Jorgensen and other authors have translated the names of materials into more commonly used language.

Jock Scott

Part of the problem with salmon fly tying is that the tyers become so obsessed with materials that they lose sight of the very act and goal of tying, which is to catch a fish. Since some materials are unavailable or are from endangered species, it is necessary to find substitutes. If these tyers do not have the exact materials called for in a classic Atlantic salmon fly dressing, they simply will not tie the fly. I argue with the purists, because it is necessary to be realistic. If you want to tie certain flies, then you have to accept the use of substitutes, some of which can be better than the materials listed in the original dressing. People who look at the flies I have tied with substitutes are often unable to tell the difference. Tyers have always looked for creative ways to fill a need—that's half of the fascination of flytying. After all, tying flies is nothing but deception. There are no rules, and when you start imposing rules, you start to limit what you can do.

Also, the fish do not notice or care which materials are in a fly. The fish are great—they are not judgmental. About ten years ago, I tied two full-dress Silver Doctors for a woman in California. I sent them to her thinking that she wanted to frame them and hang them on the wall. As it turned out, she and her husband were going to Alaska for a week of fishing. They took the flies on their trip and fished them, which was great. A couple of weeks later, she wrote me a letter to tell me that they had taken forty-one fish on these two Silver Doctors—king salmon, sockeye, rainbow, char, humpback, every fish you could find in Alaska, including northern pike. There wasn't an Atlantic salmon in the bunch, and the fish they caught did not know the Doctor was an Atlantic salmon fly. Thank goodness fish don't read.

KEITH FULSHER

EASTCHESTER, NEW YORK

I initially became interested in Atlantic salmon flies because I liked the attractive flow of the materials and of the up-eye hooks on which they were tied. These flies were different. You knew they were made to attract a very special fish. Atlantic salmon had a mystique. I had fished often for trout, even as a child in Wisconsin, where I was born and raised. The only exposure to Atlantic salmon I had was through magazine articles. I knew salmon were hard to catch. Fishing for them seemed new and different, and offered a challenge.

When I was in college in the late 1940s, I started to tie flies for a tackle shop in New York City. The shop changed its name to the Angler's Cove in the mid-1950s, relocated nearby, and hired Alex Rogan, one of the best tyers of classic Atlantic salmon flies in this country. Alex was related to the famous Irish Rogan family and, in that tradition, tied all of his flies by holding the hook in his fingers. He tied mostly classic patterns. If the shop had an order for hair-wings, I continued to get the assignment, as I had in the past, usually trading flies for equipment. It was during this period that I made my first trip to New Brunswick, Canada, to try salmon fishing. My early experiences were brief and far apart, but exciting enough to keep my interest up. It wasn't until 1963 that I started to make salmon fishing an annual affair, usually going for one or two weeks to either the Miramichi or the Cains, a major tributary of the Miramichi.

As I fished more, I grew to prefer the Cains River, a beautiful backwoods stream. The Cains was known as a "late" river because the fall run came in late. The season was open to mid-October, whereas the Miramichi closed at the end of September. There were fewer salmon in the Cains than in the Miramichi, but they were larger. In October, the foliage on the hardwood trees was gorgeous. In those days, you drove to the river on old logging roads and then hiked in the last few miles. The Cains

has a smooth surface, and the water is pure but naturally stained so dark that you can't even see your boot foot when you are standing in the waist-high water. I used to fish a pool called Ten Mile Pool, ten to fifteen miles from Doaktown. Part of the beauty was the wildlife—deer, moose, occasionally a bear. As time went on, I fished many other famous salmon rivers of New Brunswick, Newfoundland, Labrador, Iceland, and Scotland.

I became more enthusiastic about hair-wing flies in the early 1950s as I kept hearing rumors that they were outproducing feather-wing Atlantic salmon flies. I met Lew Oatman, another tyer, at one of the sports shows in New York City. He had a little office on the ninth floor of a building on Beaver Street and I was working for a bank on lower Broadway, so we often met for lunch. One day, he told me that he had tied some classic feather-wing salmon flies for a client who was going to Canada to fish the Miramichi. He threw in a small hairwing—I think it was a Cosseboom—as a gift to the client. When the client returned, he ordered lots of hair-wings because the Cosseboom was the only fly that caught fish. That story spurred me on.

Yet every time I inquired about a pattern—usually when the shop asked me to tie an unfamiliar pattern—I could never find out what was actually in it. I started a looseleaf notebook, and when I found the dressing for a pattern, I put it in the book, thinking that some day I might compile a pattern dictionary of hair-wing flies. At the Angler's Cove, I met Charlie Krom, who was starting to tie flies for the store. He also became interested in Atlantic salmon hair-wings and began to save patterns.

For twenty years, I accumulated patterns. I used to meet Joseph Bates occasionally in White Plains, New York, and at one of those get-togethers suggested that he write a book on hair-wing Atlantic salmon flies, as I thought I would never get

to it. I offered him all my patterns and notes, and he took on the job. I had a number of meetings and voluminous correspondence with him as the book developed. When his *Atlantic Salmon Flies & Fishing* was published in 1970, it didn't treat hair-wing patterns in detail the way I had anticipated, but dealt generally with all types of salmon flies. Although that was Joe's prerogative, I was still convinced there was a need for a comprehensive publica-

tion on hair-wings. I suggested to Charlie Krom that we do the book jointly. In 1981 Fly Tyer Inc. published our *Hair-Wing Atlantic Salmon Flies.*

Researching the history of the hair-wing was extremely difficult, and determining the originators of over three hundred and fifty patterns was an impossible task to accomplish with any kind of accuracy because so little was known, especially concerning early patterns. Then, too, some patterns were claimed by more than one originator. Rather than tell an inaccurate story in the book, we acknowledged that the history of pattern origination is cloudy. From my research, I believe that the hair-wing was originated in the late 1800s or early 1900s, probably in Canada, either by American or Canadian tyers and anglers, or by both working together. When I fished in Canada in the early 1960s, I met Wally Doak, Burt Miner, Jack Story, and other Canadian guides and tyers who were probably involved at the beginning of the hair-wing fly. American tyers like Herb Howard, born before the turn of the century, could also have been involved. The hair-wing was a good practical alternative for tyers in North America who knew about classic feather-wing patterns but who were unable to obtain the more exotic materials that the British had used at the turn of the century.

It is unlikely that the hair-wing was derived from the steelhead patterns of the western United States. One of the best accounts of the steelhead fly appears in Trey Combs's 1976 *Steelhead Fly Fishing and Flies*. Early steelhead flies, like early salmon flies, were converted trout flies. Information at the turn of the century did not travel readily from west to east, but rather from east to west. Atlantic salmon flies were commonly used for steelhead, and still are. Joseph Bates suggested that the hair-wing originated in England before it came to North America, but I did not find any evidence to support his theory. The English used fur for the bodies of flies, usually picked out, so that the fly was almost like a hair-wing in a reverse position. As far as I could determine, no tyer in England ever put hair on top of the fly exclusively for the wing. North American fly-tyers did, and the idea traveled back to England and is popular there today.

Hair-wings have a translucency that is very insectlike, which is why I believe that they can be more successful than the classic patterns. A great experiment could be performed by fishing for Atlantic salmon with more exact imitations of the kinds of life forms salmon see in the streambed. Lee Wulff wrote about using terrestrials to fish for Atlantic salmon. I had never tried them, but when I fished on the Nepisiguit River in New Brunswick several years ago, I made some size 16 Black Ants. Right out in the home pool at the camp was a big salmon. It would jump once in a while, but no one could raise it to a fly. I tied on an ant in a final effort on the last day of fishing and raised that fish three times. I never hooked it, but

it did come up to the fly, and each time gave it a good pull.

I am a self-taught flytyer, but if I had a problem, I would occasionally ask Lew Oatman for help in finding a solution. I did the same thing with Herb Howard and Reub Cross. Although I had experimented with flytying as a youngster, I actually taught myself how to tie from an instruction sheet that came with a flytying kit I bought from a shop in New York. I also cut apart a lot of flies, including some of Lew's—and I wish I still had those flies. I did buy materials from him. He had the best custom-dyed saddle hackle I have ever seen.

When I first started tying, I became interested in streamer flies because their sleek look appealed to me. After I met Lew, he showed me some of the patterns he was developing, which were framed and hung all over the walls of his office. Large streamer flies had become popular in Maine in the early 1900s for landlocked salmon and big brook trout. Lew probably did as much work as anyone to reduce the size of the patterns to a point where they were effective to use in the smaller, more heavily fished streams of the Northeast. A streamer or bucktail can be very successful any place where it is fished. The best fish I have caught of any kind, except steelhead, have been on what I call "minnow flies."

I tied many streamers for the Angler's Cove, and they sold well. After fishing with them, however, I felt that my flies did not come close enough to imitating baitfish. I was convinced there was a way to design a fly that more accurately resembled a minnow. I remembered the procedure of reversing bucktail to form a little ball head on a fly. I had never seen or heard of the technique being used with two or more colors. I decided to tie a dark color on top of the fly and white underneath, stretching the head out a bit. When I reversed the bucktail, I carefully controlled the two groups of fibers to create a precise division between them along the sides of the head and body of the fly. I then lacquered the heads heavily and painted an eye on each side. I tried the design on a down-eye hook, but the head was at an angle, and when I fished the fly, it failed to swim properly.

When I was in Wisconsin on a fishing trip, I went into a tackle shop and spotted some bait hooks that were offset and had long shanks and straight eyes. I adjusted the offset when I put the hook in the vise. The straight eye was perfect because I could reverse all the hair at once without any interference from the hook eye. Also, the eye blended in with the fly and became part of it, and the fly swam better in the water. The group of fifteen flies I developed in the early 1960s formed the basis of *Tying and Fishing the Thunder Creek Series*, which was published by Freshet Press in 1973. I often fish the Thunder Creek flies. The one I use the most is called the Emerald Shiner. I make it differently now. With the advent of the new synthetic materials, I use pearl Flashabou tubing, which gives the body of the fly an iridescence. I have caught Atlantic salmon on Thunder Creek patterns in New Brunswick and Iceland.

Charlie DeFeo was another tyer I met through the Angler's Cove, and I got to know him well. He was a unique painter and illustrator. I collected his flies over the years, and he created quite a few successful hair-wing patterns, a number of which are included in our book. Charlie could tie one of the best sparsely tied hair-wing flies I have ever seen. They flowed along the little size 8 or 10 hooks he used. Charlie was one of the early tyers to experiment with nymph patterns for salmon—the Silver Salmon Nymph, Gold Salmon Nymph, and others. He took the Copper Killer, a well-known salmon fly, and made it into a nymph. He would take a Jock Scott body and turn that into a nymph. I tied flies with Charlie many times. The best thing about his tying was that, once he started on salmon flies, he would get into a continuous conversation about salmon fishing. He tied fly after fly after fly, never breaking the story he was relating, and he gave each fly to a bystander. Charlie would just mesmerize you. He was a great storyteller.

I have tied a lot of feather-wing flies and still tie them as a challenge. I also tie them for fishing. I like the Black Dose, Jock Scott, and Silver Grey, and keep them in my fly box. When hair-wings don't work, I will try a feather-wing. I reduce the patterns because I am tying them on size 4s and 6s, and sometimes 8s. Other types of flies being tied today are every bit as complicated as classic Atlantic salmon flies, but tying the fully dressed traditional patterns is no longer a trade—it's an art and a form of expression. I think this approach is good for flytying. It is also good for fishing because if tyers are interested enough to tie the old patterns, whether or not they fish for Atlantic salmon, they tend to be conservation-minded and therefore lend weight to the efforts to save the Atlantic salmon and preserve its habitat.

My style of tying Atlantic salmon hair-wings and the colors I prefer have been influenced by my fishing experiences. I have found that sparsely tied flies work the best, and I like the wing to sit flat over the body and to extend no farther back than to the bend of the hook, often even shorter. I am very partial to flies with some strong blue, generally for the hackle. I also like flies with black or silver bodies, usually ribbed with silver or gold oval tinsel. I have had good luck, too, with flies that have a touch of red, as either a tip or a butt, sometimes with a strand of red fluorescent floss under the hair wing. Flies that have one or more of these features are the Red Butt Conrad, Blue Charm, Little Red Wing, and Lady Ellen. The Blue Rat has been an excellent fly for me in Newfoundland. Although I carry a complete size range of flies in single and double hooks, I like to fish mainly with singles, and size 6 is my favorite for most salmon rivers.

I enjoy designing new hair-wing patterns. When Charlie Krom and I worked on the pattern index for *Hair-Wing Atlantic Salmon Flies*, I noticed that patterns using red fox guard hair for the wings were practically nonexistent. The hair along the center of the back of a red fox is very interesting. It has a dark base, shading into a cream-colored center and ending with fiery brown tips. Several years ago I experimented with a few flies using red fox hair for winging, the hair coming from an old fox fur jacket. I decided to put some of my favorite blue in the first pattern I worked on. After many changes, a fly I call the Blue Reynard evolved. It worked, so I expanded the Reynard series to include a black, orange, green, and yellow version, all with the same general styling and red fox for the wing. Touches of color make the difference in the patterns.

Alex Rogan once said something I have never forgotten. His job at the Angler's Cove was to turn out flies, so to avoid distracting conversations with customers, he tied his flies in a private room at the back of the shop. He would occasionally call me to the back room and give me some pointers. I remember him saying when he related some of his teaching experiences, "You know, I've learned more from amateurs than they've ever learned from me." That's the truest statement in flytying I have ever heard. Someone who considers himself or herself to be a professional often doesn't have the time, or want to take the time, to experiment. The amateur is always experimenting, always searching for an easier way to do something. The amateurs are the ones who, in my view, are creating all the new techniques and the new interest in flytying. That is the challenge of flytying—there is always something different to try out.

RON ALCOTT

GROTON, MASSACHUSETTS

The term "art" has been applied to flytying as far back as the early nineteenth century. Art is a talent acquired and enhanced through learning and experience. Craft is more a trade that requires a particular skill. Flytying involves both, but it is definitely an art. Everyone has a gift, and I am fortunate to have discovered that tying Atlantic salmon flies is my gift and my form of artistic expression.

My goal has never been to seek fame in flytying for its own sake but my primary motivation is to be remembered. To accomplish that, it is necessary to have a broad familiarity with the subject. Much more important, a tyer must be willing to share that knowledge with others—to be remembered for giving something. Teaching is an important way to be accessible to others. For the instructor, it has additional advantages such as the self-esteem and recognition one enjoys from helping people tie a fly that comes out right. They never dreamed they could tie a salmon fly and are awed at the results, and I feel good sharing my knowledge with them. I cannot speak for other flytyers who

LEFT **_Colonel's Lady_**

teach, but I am simultaneously humbled and flattered to receive the ultimate compliment from a class of tyers—that they want to know what I know and want to have the opportunity to emulate my style of tying.

Although Atlantic salmon flies are my only interest now, my first attempts at flytying were trout flies. In the early 1970s, a half-dozen local shops had a desperate need for flies and gave me orders for dry flies, wet flies, and streamers. One day a shop owner called me with a huge order—for one hundred forty-four gross of three patterns. He gave me two years to finish them and was going to pay me the awesome price of twenty-five cents per fly. When I informed him that my time was worth more than seventy-five cents an hour, he told me, "I

have tyers producing these flies in five minutes." I said, "I don't tie like that." The situation was so discouraging that I stopped tying until 1982.

For ten years, my flytying materials and tools were stored away in a closet. One day I pulled them down and thought of trying to tie some of the flies in Joseph Bates's _Atlantic Salmon Flies & Fishing._ Atlantic salmon flies—the techniques for tying the flies and the range of unusual materials used to tie them presented an unquestionable challenge. I was rusty after all those years and was very unhappy with the results of my tying. I had a contemporary book on flytying but found that the techniques did not work for me. Questions surfaced: What is Indian crow? What is speckled bustard? Pig's wool? None of my friends had the answers.

From the list of names and addresses in the appendix of Joe Bates's book, I wrote to a historian in Scotland and asked him how long it would take a person to become a "master flytyer." He wrote back that I would need to devote ten or fifteen years. It was a little late for me to contribute that much time to it, so I decided to take a year off from work to practice tying and to study the Atlantic salmon fly. During that year, if I was not tying flies eight hours a day, I could be found at a museum or library reading and researching.

My efforts reached the point where I could talk with ornithologists in a museum using the Latin _Rupicola sanguinolenta_ and _Rupicola rupicola_ instead of red cock-of-the-rock and orange cock-of-the-rock. I even wrote to Dr. Jean Delacour, the world-famous French aviculturist and author of numerous books. Before World War II, he had Indian crow in his collection in France, but lost them all during the war. He referred me to a zoo for more information. The zoo curator was surprised that I had written the famous Dr. Delacour and was even more astonished that I had received an answer. By the end of the year, people were telling me that the information I had accumulated helped to answer questions they had wondered about for years.

In July of 1983, I was able to go to Scotland for the first time. After reading about Megan Boyd in Joe Bates's book, I wanted to meet her. On our way up to Brora, I said to my host, "How should I act around Megan?" He said, "Just be yourself." So I thought I would go for broke. When we arrived at Megan's bungalow in Brora, they said to Megan, "Ron came over yesterday and kept asking, 'When are you going to take me to see Megan?'" They went on like that for two or three minutes. "Well, Megan," I said, "that's not entirely the way it happened. True, I did arrive yesterday and they kept telling me, 'We're going to take you up to meet Megan Boyd.' I said, 'Who's Megan Boyd?'" She really laughed when she heard that and we have been dear friends ever since. You can just be yourself with Megan because she is so comfortable with herself.

I sat in Megan's tying room and watched her tie flies. Her approach was much different from mine and the other tyers I knew. She tied fishing flies, not exhibition flies. Megan did not use a bobbin—she "couldn't be bothered." That was her philosophy. She worked for so many years without light that when she finally had electricity installed in her bungalow, she often forgot to turn on the lights. Megan is a great teacher in that if you asked her to critique a fly, she was never intimidated by who you were and would tell you exactly what she thought of your tying. Megan taught me a lot about the symmetry of flies. We shared opinions, and sometimes debated them. She did not like the shade of blue feather I was using. Hers was lighter and more subtle. We also compared patterns. The fly that most interested me when I went to Scotland was the Sutherland, and Megan was able to give me the dressing for it from memory. We talked about different writers, mostly Pryce-Tannatt because his book was the one Megan used and so do I most of the time. We agreed that he had modernized salmon fly tying for the twentieth century.

Shortly after meeting Megan, I met Joe Bates. We exchanged a lot of thoughts on the techniques used by early flytyers and on the history and origins of salmon flies. I tied Atlantic salmon flies for his collection and in return he gave me some very nice items in trade. I am very fond of Joe's wife Helen. One day in 1985, I took a Lady Amherst fly to Joe. Helen really liked the Lady Amherst pheasant feathers. Whereas tyers were always giving their flies to Joe, I thought of tying one just for her using the Lady Amherst pheasant. The feather really isn't black and white. It's green and white, but the green is so dark that it looks black. I selected claret silk for the body since it contrasts so well with the black, or green, and white. After experimenting with other materials, I fell in love with the blue and white spots of the Kenya crested guinea fowl for the throat of the fly.

In the back of my mind, I also wanted to prove a point. Joe felt that tyers today should not design Atlantic salmon flies because there are already so many patterns. When the fly was finished, I went to visit Joe and Helen and gave the fly to Helen. She was ecstatic. She was also surprised at the name until I reminded her that, while Joe was on active duty in the army, she was always addressed in the army tradition as the "Colonel's Lady." "You're right," she said. "They did call me the Colonel's Lady." Joe put the fly on the mantle, and we had lunch. After lunch, I walked with Joe back into the living room and he said, "You know, that's a handsome fly." I thanked him.

As proud as I am of the Colonel's Lady, I think the Jock Scott best expresses my capabilities as a flytyer. With its more than fifty individual pieces of materials, it's a complicated pattern to tie. People often ask me how to tie Jock Scotts or other flies of the same pattern so that they look identical. Knowing the functional and technical aspects of the proportions of a salmon fly comes from observation and experience. Even though I have been tying salmon flies for almost ten years, I never guess the proportions for a particular pattern and always measure the components and their relative placement on the hook. I also tell tyers that they need to discipline themselves to retie a part of the fly until they are completely satisfied with the results. The greatest difficulty in learning how to tie is knowing when to repeat a step in order to make the fly turn out well, rather than rushing through it with the hope that the finished fly will look good. A fly should never be allowed to become a reject. It is better to correct mistakes during the tying process instead of compounding the errors.

Another reason I am drawn to the Jock Scott is its intriguing history. All tyers and many nontyers know the fly, and its fame has made it synonymous with Atlantic salmon flies. There are numerous legends about the fly, many of them romantic and only few of them verifiable. In *The Art of the Atlantic Salmon Fly*, Joe Bates reprints the obituary of Jock Scott published in the February 18, 1893, issue of *The Field*. The

Jock Scott

writer, using the pen name of Punt Gun, describes how Jock Scott, while working for Lord John Scott, tied the fly in 1850. Jock Scott was so pleased with the fly that he gave it—as yet unnamed—to John Forrest, a maker of fishing tackle in Kelso on the River Tweed in England. Forrest had such success fishing with the fly that he named it for Jock Scott, the inventor. By the time of Jock Scott's death, the fly was famous.

In his book of 1895, *The Salmon Fly*, George Kelson prints a letter he received from the same person who wrote the obituary under the name of Punt Gun. Claiming to know Jock Scott well, Punt Gun said he had a Jock Scott fly given to him by its inventor, who told him of its origin in 1850. A black and white photograph of the Jock Scott fly appears in Sir Herbert Maxwell's

Salmon and Sea Trout, published three years after Kelson's book. The caption identifies the fly as the original one first dressed by Jock Scott, but states that he tied it, not in 1850, but in 1845, on his way to Norway in the service of Lord John Scott. The authenticity of the fly and story in Maxwell's book cannot be confirmed, and the weight of Punt Gun's familiarity with Jock Scott and his life tips the scales in favor of what he wrote.

I believe that Jock Scott originated his fly in 1850 and that his station and perhaps his modesty prevented him from naming it after himself. John Forrest of Kelso took care of that. The Jock Scott I tie is very much a twentieth century interpretation, but in its heritage and its design, it is the ultimate Atlantic salmon fly.

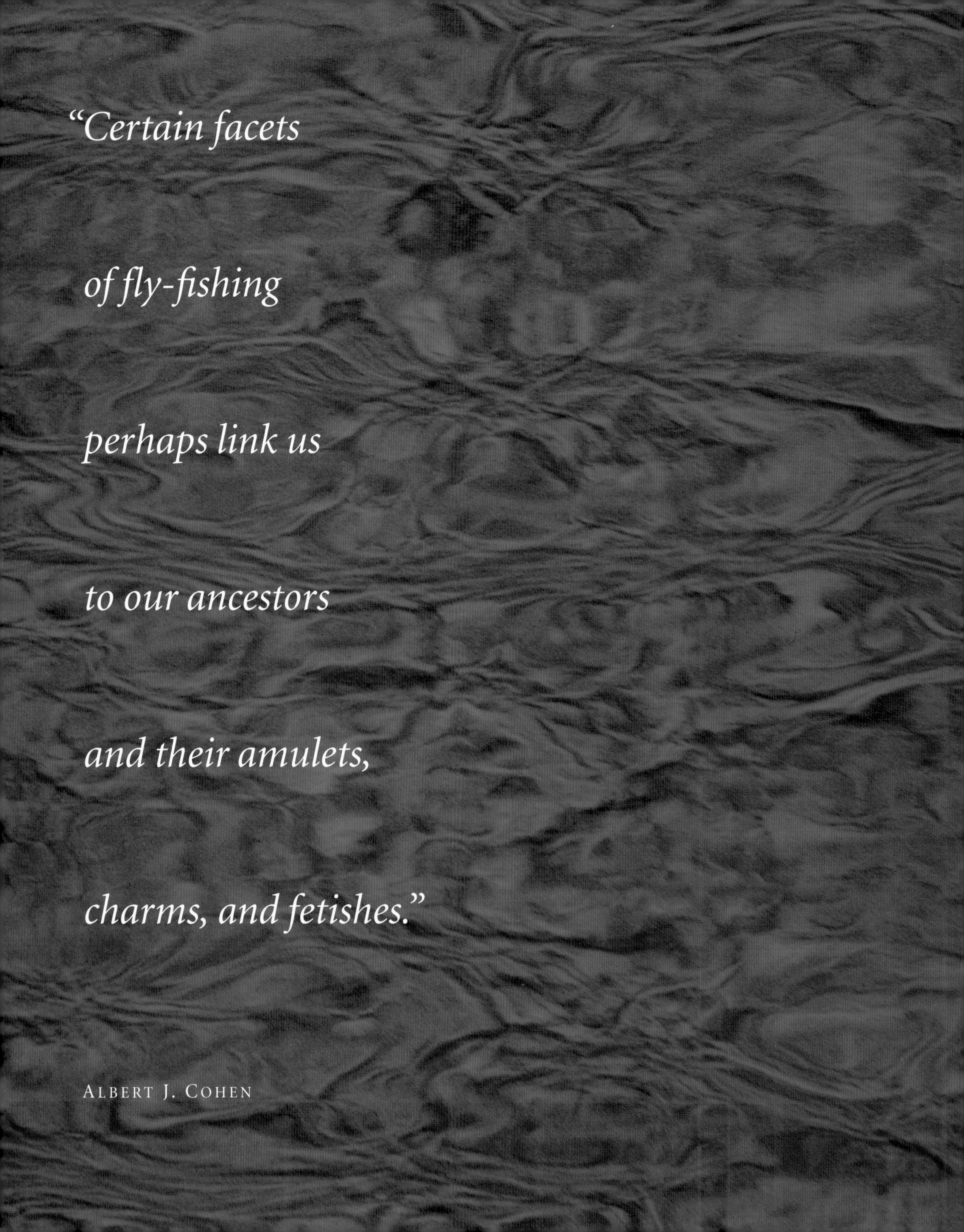

"Certain facets

of fly-fishing

perhaps link us

to our ancestors

and their amulets,

charms, and fetishes."

ALBERT J. COHEN

Western United States

ALBERT J. COHEN

*Unnamed Patterns
from the
Nineteenth Century*

STEVE FERNANDEZ

Easy Off

Pompadour

Untitled

JUDY LEHMBERG

Evening Star

WAYNE LUALLEN

Nicholson

Quilled Eagle

JOHN VAN DERHOOF

Gordon

Moonlight

TED NIEMEYER

Belle Series

MARVIN NOLTE

Ballyshannon

Dusty Miller

ERIC OTZINGER

Bonanza

Niagara

ALBERT J. COHEN

DALLAS, TEXAS

Even though we think we live in what are the most modern of times, we are not that far removed from our ancestors of a not-so-distant past, and in many respects our fly-fishing behavior demonstrates this. Many of us are fascinated by fly-fishing and its related accoutrements. But have we considered that certain facets of fly-fishing—the sometimes superstitious and ritualistic behavior of the fisherman, the mystique surrounding the choice of fly patterns, the use of furs, hairs, and feathers—perhaps, just perhaps, link us to our ancestors and their amulets, charms, and fetishes.

Fly dressing has a storied past and a longstanding tradition. I find more satisfaction in dressing a fly that has a historic basis and a connection with the past than in tying one that does not. Although a great many salmon fly patterns have been documented in books and periodicals, there are probably many more patterns and variations which have not. Fly dressers of the past, like those today, had their own patterns which they hoped would result in more effective lures, and which, perhaps in a Merlin-esque way, often had secret combinations of components or included hard-to-obtain materials endowed with some special fish-catching capability.

LEFT: *Unnamed Pattern from the Nineteenth Century*

The flies shown here are based, as far as I know, on undocumented antiques, one from my own collection and the others borrowed from friends in Scotland and Houston, Texas. I do not even know the names of these flies, or even if they ever had names. The materials I used are identical, for the most part, to those in the antiques. As fly dressers have always done, and because I thought changes would improve the flies, I made a few modifications using alternate materials—silk floss for seal's fur and teal for snipe—and chose other colors for the body hackle and throat of one fly, and added cheeks on another. In dressing the flies, I followed styles of the period, and as did the Victorian and Edwardian fly dressers, I ordered the juxtaposition of the wing components as I saw fit. By dressing these antique patterns, I feel they have been entered into the stream of history for future generations.

The history of fly-fishing and especially the history of the evolution of the fly began to interest me as I became more involved with Atlantic salmon flies. In 1986, Ron Alcott introduced me to Joseph Bates. Joe had an extensive collection of flies from all over the world and certainly, to my knowledge, had the largest collection of Atlantic salmon flies in the United States that was made available for people to examine. When I saw his collection, I realized that the flies not only were collectible but were fascinating from an evolutionary point of view. Not all of Joe's flies were exhibition quality—some had been fished, a few were damaged by moths—but the older flies had the appealing patina of age and history.

Joe also showed me his library, which included more than the commonly sought-after books containing information on salmon flies. At that time, I had only a dozen books or so, and as a result of seeing Joe's library and long discussions with him about the importance of history, I began to acquire more books in order to try to understand the early authors and what they were attempting to accomplish. I was obsessed with salmon flies. If a book contained other subjects, I didn't read about them—I would just turn to the section on salmon flies.

When I first began to dress salmon flies in the mid-1980s, I read about patterns and tying techniques in the books by George Kelson, T. E. Pryce-Tannatt, and J. H. Hale. I approached the tying of a salmon fly the same way as I would a trout fly. Looking back, I feel that I really didn't understand what I was doing or why I was doing it. For some reason, I was convinced that there were rules of some sort for dressing these flies. During 1985, I took a weekend class in Dallas from Wayne Luallen, visited with Bob Veverka and Bill Hunter on the east coast, and took several lessons with Ron Alcott in Massachusetts. I wrote long letters and spoke on the telephone with Ron and Wayne, attempting to reconcile their advice and trying to understand the requisite techniques.

I believe that the turning point came in early 1986 when I was unable to tie for three months. This allowed me to concentrate on reading, and I began to understand—at least, I think I began to understand—what the historic authors were attempting to do. As I went further, and also after seeing many antique flies, it became apparent that a tremendous amount of fly-dressing history, possibly the majority of it, was not recorded, and as a result, much today is subject to conjecture and speculation. After thinking about the concepts of rules and proportions for dressing salmon flies, and reading the books, and looking at the plates and artistic renditions of flies, along with studying the antique flies I had acquired, I realized that the historic authors did just about anything they thought would make the flies more effective for catching salmon (or fishermen's money, as the case may be) and used whatever materials they had available. Many fishermen of that time referred to their flies as "lures," since these concoctions had no counterpart in nature. Since the salmon fly is but a figment of human imagination and has little resemblance to any living creature, I believe that any concepts of rules and proportions are nothing more than preposterous attempts at promulgating what never existed or could ever exist—sheer poppycock!

It is entirely possible that when Victorian authors wrote books and articles in periodicals, they may have taken a look at their fly boxes or notes at the time they were preparing their manuscripts and thought, "That's an effective salmon fly. I'll write about it," then described the pattern at hand. But does anyone believe that George Kelson's dressings of Champions or James Wright's of Silver Greys or Daniel O'Fee's of Doherty's Judges, for example, were each dressed with identical components, in the same style, and in the same proportions? That assumption would be naive. The more I looked at the subject and the more I read, the more I came to the conclusion that the only rule for tying Atlantic salmon flies was that the fly had to be dressed on a hook of some sort.

Considering that the history of dressing Atlantic salmon flies is, at the same time, vague and precise (in that most patterns specify certain materials), my approach to tying an Atlantic salmon fly involves considerable conceptual work. I look at a particular pattern, including any similar antiques I have, and read all the different commentators' views of that pattern. A salmon fly of the same name, such as the Black Dog or the Shannon, will have a number of different patterns, sometimes with radically different materials. I determine which one suits my fancy, whether it is from Francis, Hale, Hardy, Kelson, Blacker, or whomever. Selecting the dressing gives me a feel for the particular style I will follow because the fly was usually dressed during different periods of time, generally beginning in the nineteenth century, and the styles and, in some cases, the materials of each period and of each author were different. As I develop a fly, I eliminate some preconceived ideas and change and modify my thoughts accordingly, until I have a fly that flows and seems coherent to me. It is a kind of ritual, and I think that, as I get older, I am becoming more and more ritualistic.

Once I decide which pattern I am going to dress and how I am going to tie it, I might do the tag and tail over one weekend, then do the body and underwing the same weekend or a

ABOVE:

Unnamed
Pattern
from the
Nineteenth
Century

week later. A couple of weeks later, I may do the main wing. If I am pleased with where a feather is in relationship to the rest of the fly, I let it be. I always have a bodkin in my hand to rearrange the feathers and position them where I want them, or a razor blade in order to redo a particular step or even the entire fly. I am not in a hurry. Finishing a fly is an instantaneous moment. It's the process of getting there that is the most rewarding. Once the fly is completed, what else is there to do? Very few of my own salmon flies are on display. I find that looking at my flies is not nearly as enjoyable or as fulfilling as dressing them. There are so many things in life people look forward to getting behind them. Dressing a salmon fly should not be one of them.

My catharsis is fishing, but because I do not have the time to fish very often, my connection to the sport is reading and studying angling history. After a few years of extensive reading, I realized that the history of fishing flies in general is much more compelling than the evolution of the salmon fly alone. There are more styles, the flies are older, there are many more commentators to read, and the body of literature is much broader. For several years I was fascinated by nineteenth and early twentieth century British and Irish authors. I have read quite a bit of Frederic Halford and G.E.M. Skues, and I collect flies from the related time periods. I like to read George Kelson's weekly columns in the *Fishing Gazette* and *Land and Water*.

I also became interested in the evolution of fly-fishing in the United States after reading Paul Schullery's *American Fly Fishing* and then began to read the nineteenth and early twentieth century American authors such as Theodore Gordon, Thaddeus Norris, James Henshall, Frank Forester, Edward Hewitt, Louis Rhead, and George La Branche. Through their writings, I grew to appreciate how they thought about flies and fishing, and about the fishing problems they were trying to overcome. Sometimes I try to imagine myself as a fisherman living during those times and reading these authors to learn about fishing methods and techniques.

Studying and attempting to understand our heritage, and sometimes even fishing the old fly patterns, are like sipping a fine, aged brandy—very mellowing and gratifying. It is unfortunate that many people never attempt the study either because they do not care or because they cannot find the time. "The modern possessors of genius—and in this precocious age of ours there are many," William Shipley once mused, "disdain . . . to wend their way along the old and beaten roads, and will not condescend to travel in pursuit of knowledge unless in [first] class . . . of some rapid . . . [transit]. . . . To them our ancestors seem slow coaches in everything. . . ." This observation of how little human behavior changes appeared in Shipley's *A True Treatise on the Art of Fly-Fishing, Trolling, Etc.*, written in 1838.

STEVE FERNANDEZ

RESEDA, CALIFORNIA

I cannot remember a time in my life when I wasn't designing or modifying something. I suppose I will never be able to leave well enough alone. When I was young and could not spend thirty dollars on whatever widget I needed, I would make it. A two-by-four, some wire, and a couple of pieces of paper worked sufficiently for my needs. When I overhauled my car, I made some of the tools. As I got older, I could afford the utilitarian item, but if a well-crafted object was important, I preferred to create it. Part of my esthetic attitude stems from my education in architecture, when I started to look at buildings differently. What is the reason to have a pitched roof? To shed water. Is that the only way to shed water? How can I change the esthetics of the roof but still give it the same function?

In 1980, when I entered architecture school, I stopped tying Atlantic salmon flies. When I started to tie them again in 1983, my attitude toward them had changed. Many more tyers were interested in salmon flies than when I tied them in the mid-1970s, and were approaching them as works of art rather than as fishing flies. They put them in a box, hung them on the wall, and called them art. Flytyers spoke about the creativity involved in tying salmon flies. I understood what they meant. Tying a salmon fly requires that a tyer be very proficient at manipulating materials and the proportions used in a fly, and that a tyer understand the history of the salmon fly. My exposure to contemporary art and architecture, at home and then at school, had a tremendous impact on me, and I applied this to flytying. If an Atlantic salmon fly is an art form, then why not really treat it as an art instead of retying old patterns?

My interest in salmon fly tying was renewed, but rather than doing something subtle, I went to the extreme end of the spectrum. I started with a hook. Since I wasn't going to fish with it, I straightened it out completely. I used standard Atlantic salmon fly materials—golden pheasant, dyed goose, jungle cock—but attached them to the hook in a very atypical fashion. Although there was seemingly no order, the order was free-form. The lacquer on a fly is used in one particular position, on the head. Why limit it to one area? So I made a pattern of little epoxy dots along the shank. The fly had tags and tips, but they were not at the bend of the hook, because none of the hooks had a bend.

I decided to show five of these flies at the conclave of the Southwest Council of the Federation of Fly Fishers in Los Angeles in the spring of 1983. I put three of them in a little jet black cardboard box. The box had windows and was lit from above. The flies looked very stark against the black background. At the conclave, I demonstrated the flies I always do—the Royal Wulff, Adams, Irresistible, Muddler—because people usually have technical questions about the trout flies they commonly tie and I like to help them. I placed the black box next to me on the table, and everybody who saw the flies, with three exceptions, shook their heads and walked away. I suspect that I may have trampled on the sensitivities of those people, who thought I hated Atlantic salmon flies. That wasn't how I felt at all. I love salmon flies. My intention was to radically change the attitude with which salmon flies were made, used, and observed, while staying within the realm of Atlantic salmon fly tying. The flies might have been a little satirical, but with affection. I thought hard about what I was doing and deliberately made that statement as my reintroduction to tying salmon flies.

That first work was didactic, without question, but it had to be because I was trying to make a point. Atlantic salmon flies are very involved with tradition. What do tyers interested in salmon flies study? They study what is available—the history. Trout flies, on the other hand, carry a less overtly esthetic attitude about what they should look like. They usually imitate something very specific—an insect, for example. Their purpose is to catch fish. Atlantic salmon flies are not imitative. They are flights of fancy. The prevailing attitude behind them is to work within tradition to make a beautiful, technically correct fly. It's wonderful to see tyers who are steeped in a purist approach to Atlantic salmon flies. If they want to be traditionalists, that's fine. But I am not a traditionalist. I don't tie a salmon fly the way it was once tied. Atlantic salmon fly tying is very revivalist. It signifies a wish for bygone days. The past seems so pleasing that people want to replicate it. There are other things that interest me.

I currently work on the periphery of the full-dress salmon fly. The point of view is more implicit and less didactic. I don't necessarily begin with a particular statement or follow a particular methodology, because that limits my spontaneity. There is a lot of chance involved, which I used to discount because it seemed that I wasn't in control of what I was doing. Yet I now think that I am in control since I rely strongly on experimentation and intuition. It is hard to define the exact process, but from all the experiences and images I have collected, something emerges.

I cannot imagine myself tying the way I do now without first having gone to the extreme I did in 1983. I knew that I would not continue to work with the ideas in those early flies because I wanted to remain within flytying, which means that the flies must have hooks. When I tie a fly, I still manipulate the hook, but not to such an extreme. Some of the hooks are contemporary 1/0 "Bartleets" that have been reshaped and the barbs removed. To create a totally different shape, I use piano wire. This allows me to exaggerate certain parts of the hook or create a shape that is difficult to make by modifying an existing hook. Since the altered "Bartleets" have to be refinished, I am free to choose any color I like, such as a clear coat of lacquer over bright bare steel or white splatter paint over a blue-gray background.

The style of fly that began in 1987 with the Pompadour necessitated drawing. Before I tied the Pompadour, or even named it, I made a sketch to create a high hump on an Atlantic salmon fly wing. Then I manipulated a feather to produce a certain arch in it. I kept working with the feather until suddenly I arrived at an extreme curve. This was *very* interesting, and it became the Pompadour. I still often start with a draw-

ing, where I design a wing curve that becomes the basis for the esthetics of a fly. I can design a fly quickly in a drawing, rather than by tying, which would take far longer. The drawing is often easy to do, but making a feather follow the shape in a drawing is very difficult. When the drawing is translated into a fly, it sometimes loses a lot of zip, and the idea exists better as a drawing than as a fly. I don't mind that, because it may lead to another idea. I have to be able to follow through on a fly and allow myself to realize that it might be a mistake. I want to see where the mistake might lead me. If you don't make mistakes, you're not really going forward.

Some of my flies reflect Pop Art attitudes. I think there is value in taking an image from everyday life and using it artistically. We take so much of what we see and do for granted, yet something as seemingly senseless as the jingle for the Easy-Off oven cleaner commercial has impact on us. By examining these commonplace elements, I discover ideas in the rough. Objects not normally thought of as being beautiful may become so. Pop artist Claes Oldenburg is thought of as being humorous but there is important value behind his work, as in his *Batcolumn* in Chicago in front of the social security office. Baseball is popular among the economic strata of people who use the building. Then there is the material. The bat is made from crisscrossed stainless steel, which refers to the construction of a certain skyscraper in Chicago, and is seen in the context of the nearby highrises. The piece works well on a number of levels.

Easy Off started as a Pop idea and is both humorous and serious. The spots appearing to come off the wing of the fly suggest that the wing is being cleaned. The name Easy Off occurred to me when I decided to paint white spots on a black hook, like the pattern on the inside of an oven. On that level the fly is tongue in cheek, a bit corny, but I try to transcend the corniness by combining elements of traditional Spey and Dee styles of tying in a fly that also has a very high wing. The wing bulges forward, over the eye of the hook, and forms a continuous curve that carries through the throat and the horns, which are tied under rather than above the hook. The bare hook serves as the body of the fly, and the splatter pattern substitutes for the floss and tinsel in a traditional pattern. I flared the tail to give it a greater presence next to the wing.

I often take an unusual approach to materials. Both Easy Off and Pompadour have wings with extreme shapes.

ABOVE:
Untitled

ABOVE:

Pompadour

ABOVE:

Easy Off

Pompadour has a tarnished tinsel body. Flytyers normally throw tarnished tinsel away, but the golds and blues that developed as the tinsel tarnished are quite beautiful. I discovered that floss makes an excellent dubbing material when I was tying a Green Highlander and lacked the correct green seal's fur. I remembered that the end of a broken strand of floss looked like seal's fur, so I cut up some floss, put it into the blender, and dubbed it on the fly. It was sensational. I also use it extensively for the bodies of nymphs. I haven't used seal's fur since.

I am constantly trying to make materials do what they are not normally used for in a fly. I attempt to get technique to work for me, but do not want it to be the primary focus. I do not want to marry a wing, strip by strip, just to show off my skill, though I am always woodshedding. I tied the tag on the Pompadour over and over until I was fairly satisfied with it, but that wasn't important to the kernel of the idea. Although technique supports idea and can be the springboard for idea, it is more of a tool. It is easy to get buried in technique and lose the idea. While the shape of the wing is crucial to my flies, absolute perfection is not. I am reminded of an architect named Kazunari Sakamoto who went so far as to use a sloppy contractor to execute one of his buildings to see if the ideas still held up. They did.

One of the benefits of commercial tying is that you learn about technique. For nine years, beginning when I was fifteen years old, I tied flies for Ned Grey's shop in Montrose, north of Los Angeles. I often tied twenty to forty dozen flies a week, which gave me an incredible amount of practice. A commercial tyer has to tie proficiently and quickly to make money and stay ahead of fly orders. Making the most attractive fly is not the point. That is a legitimate attitude for a commercial tyer, but I like to tie an esthetically pleasing fly, and I enjoy fishing with a well-tied classic trout fly. Even when I stopped tying salmon flies in the early 1980s, I continued to tie trout flies. I would play around with trout flies to make them float better, experiment with materials, or design a different wing. I put my Adams away and filled my fly boxes with Wickham's Fancies because I was interested in them.

Although I tied traditional Atlantic salmon flies in the mid-1970s, I seldom tie them now. Last year I tied a Jock Scott, which for me is *very* traditional, so I took license with the pattern. Spey hackle replaced the customary hackle, the horns and jungle cock were underneath the hook instead of on top of it, the wing had a high arch, and the color strips in the wing extended past the tail like eyelashes. The closest I now come to tying a traditional Atlantic salmon fly is the Albino Underhanded Ranger. This allows me to remain within tradition while also exploring my own territory. My version of the Durham Ranger has counterparts to what is in the classic fly, but I use a white hook, pale materials such as cream floss and bleached golden pheasant tippets, and Spey hackle.

It is not enough for me to rearrange the feathers on a fly, as I did with the Jock Scott. Doing something familiar is comfortable and easy. For me, however, that is uncomfortable. I am often uneasy about my creations—but uneasiness is a necessity for the process of creation. I constantly listen to a wide range of music, even when I tie flies. But it is the spirit of Eric Dolphy and Thelonious Monk that helps me overcome my inhibitions about creating something different. When they play with atonality and dissonance, it is unexpected and beautiful. They sound so free. I am not trying to be different for the sake of being different. I am trying to be different as a way to create new things. I am always searching for new ideas.

JUDY LEHMBERG

DAYTON, TEXAS

I have loved nature ever since I was a child growing up in a suburb of Fort Worth. There were great expanses of open space with fields and creeks to explore, and I was always out collecting crawdads, tadpoles, and other creatures. Opossums, horny toads, turtles, birds, mice—I would find them and bring them home for a while, then let them go. Even at an early age, I knew that I wanted to study biology. During the summer between ninth and tenth grades, I went to Puerto Rico, where I practically lived in the water, exploring the coral reefs with all their diverse organisms. It seemed inevitable that I would go on to study biology, botany, and zoology.

What later interested me about flytying were the natural materials used to make the flies. When I met Verne, who later became my husband and who fished, fishing or tying flies didn't appeal to me, but the materials in his flytying kit did. Being a biologist and a pack rat, I was fascinated by all the specimens in the Herter's catalogs of flytying supplies. I just wanted to have an Arctic fox tail, a mole skin, a coyote tail, or any other "souvenir" that caught my eye. Then, in the late 1970s, Verne started to teach me how to tie trout flies. He showed me the basic techniques and patterns since he was tying mostly Humpies, Royal Wulffs, and other attractor flies for trout. I enjoyed the tying, and looking back on it, I realize that it was inevitable I'd eventually tie flies and find someone who would fish them.

Verne made his big error when he started to teach me to fly-fish, because then I tied fewer flies for him. I went to Paradise Valley in Montana and took a weekend fly-fishing course on the well-known spring creeks with George Anderson and Doug Swisher. That was the beginning—I got bit. Once I learned to fish, tying flies began to make more sense. Even though I had tied flies by the time I went to Montana, I was not knowledgeable about the insects found on a trout stream and lacked the experience to know what qualities were necessary to put into a fly. From looking at pictures in books, I was aware of the proportions that trout flies should have, but I essentially tied flies that appealed to me. Fishing the spring creeks made me want to collect aquatic insects, study them, and try to imitate them.

When I first saw Atlantic salmon flies, I thought they were the gaudiest, ugliest flies I had ever seen. Why would anyone want to put all that stuff on a hook and waste so much time doing it? That's not the way a fly is supposed to look. I had a set idea in my mind that flies should be made with natural-colored materials and should imitate actual insects. What changed my opinion about salmon flies was discovering all of the unusual materials from which they are made. Still being a pack rat, I wanted to add them to my collection. I was also challenged by the difficulty of getting so many materials onto a hook in the correct manner. Every summer Verne and I would go fishing for trout in Montana, so in 1983 I decided to take a class on Atlantic salmon flies with Jim Carpenter and Bill Blackstone at the national conclave of the Federation of Fly Fishers in West Yellowstone. After that, I knew I had to buy all the materials. For me that was the enjoyable part. Tying the flies became more and more involving, and the next year I took another class at the national conclave, with Wayne Luallen, John Van Derhoof, and Dave McNeese.

Even though I have tied salmon flies for almost ten years, I pay more attention to color and materials than to the history of the fly I am tying. Atlantic salmon flies are steeped in tradition, and many tyers are consumed with learning about that history. That's their preference. I look at the historical books not to read about the past but to discover a new pattern I want to tie or to find out how a traditional fly was done. I start by reading the materials in the fly dressings because there are certain feathers I want to use for a wing or for the hackle. Then I consider the shades of color in the pattern and try to assemble the fly in my mind. I may not make an exact copy of a known pattern since I enjoy coming up with a different interpretation of a dressing. After all, the challenge of salmon flies was what interested me in the first place. When I first bought Alec Jackson's gold hooks, I designed my own flies rather than use the traditional dressings in books. Yellows, oranges, and reds are compatible with the warm tones of gold, and I experimented with creating patterns I had never seen before.

It is not necessary, I feel, to be true to one source of patterns for salmon flies. I am not opposed to combining in one fly the components from dressings of different eras—the hackle from a Kelson dressing of one hundred years ago and the wing from a Pryce-Tannatt dressing from earlier in this century. Kelson, Pryce-Tannatt, Hale, Taverner—I incorporate whatever sounds workable, keeping in mind that they were the writers who wrote down the patterns, but also that there had to be many ways of tying an Atlantic salmon fly or there wouldn't be such variations among the traditional patterns and styles. Tying salmon flies does not require the number of rules that people may think it does. Some important aspects of life need to have rules, but tying Atlantic salmon flies is not one of them.

My interest in wildlife motivates me to be environmentally conscious. In my flytying, I don't want to use materials from endangered species. Many tyers do, and that aspect of tying Atlantic salmon flies bothers me. I would rather have feathers from domestically raised jungle cock than know I took the feathers from the next to the last jungle cock in the wild. Verne jokes with me and calls my attitude "situation ethics." In some areas of life, I apply situation ethics, but this is

OPPOSITE:

Evening Star

not one of them. One of my main beliefs is that everything has a right to be on this earth—and when I say that I mean animals as well as human beings.

Some tyers decline to tie a pattern unless they have the materials used in salmon flies a hundred years ago. I try to obtain as good a substitute as I can, and I may use a feather that is not listed in a traditional dressing. The authors who originally wrote the fly dressings in the books used today were not so fanatical about materials. They had access to certain feathers, and they probably used substitutes that they talked about but never wrote about. It seems to me that those early tyers had more time than anything else and happened to be the ones to write down the dressings for what later became classic salmon flies. Who's to say what flies other people tied but did not record? They might have thought that Kelson and the other writers were the oddballs of the salmon fly business.

When I demonstrate tying Atlantic salmon flies, people come up and start talking to me. They think they can get a rise out of me by saying, "Are you going to fish that fly?" That doesn't bother me a bit. I have fished Atlantic salmon flies only for bass because fishing for Atlantic salmon is so expensive. I just go along with them and say, "Yes, you can use it for bass, crappie, or trout, or anything you want." I can tell that what I said disappoints them. The only salmon fly of mine that I know has been fished was used by a friend who travels frequently and took one of my Blue Doctors to Great Britain. He wrote me a little biography about what my fly did while it was there. It was fished in the rivers Spey, Dee, and Don. On the Spey, it was cast with a fifteen-foot Spey rod. On the Dee, it was fished by the blue-blooded son of a baronet who happened to be a doctor. Through its travels, the Blue Doctor remained unbloodied. I plan to add to the fly's biography by

finding people who are fishing for Atlantic salmon outside the United States and sending the Doctor with them to see how long it can keep circulating, and if it can catch fish.

Although my favorite type of fishing is for trout, I will continue to tie Atlantic salmon flies. Tying salmon flies involves a different mind-set from tying trout flies. I am tying for the person—to please a human audience—rather than for the fish. I am egotistical enough to enjoy it when people watch me tie. I also like teaching, which is what I do for a living. If you act enthusiastic about a subject I can teach you—be it flytying or biology—you won't be able to get away from me because I will talk your ear off. You don't have to give me much encouragement.

What also motivates me to tie Atlantic salmon flies is that I will never tie a perfect one. There will always be new materials and new arrangements to try. My style will probably change. That evolution is visible in the work of other tyers, and I have been waiting for it to happen in mine. Although people tell me how interesting it is to watch my tying progress over the years, I am unable see the changes. I saved a couple of my Atlantic salmon flies from several years ago, and the differences between them and the flies I tie now are in quality, not in style. I know what I am seeking to achieve in a salmon fly and I haven't been able to create the right one yet. One of my earlier flies is framed and hanging in my home. Every morning I look at it and think that I should throw it away. It makes me mad to see it. There are a dozen different things that I do not like about that fly. I go through the same thought process every day, and I guess I keep the fly to remind myself that I can do better.

WAYNE LUALLEN

It amazes me that in recent years so many people have become involved in the revival of tying and collecting Atlantic salmon flies, and the popularity shows little sign of waning. In the late 1970s, when this renewed interest in salmon flies began, I felt that it would be a fad, just as many specific materials and designs for trout flies were fads and later fell by the wayside. My interest in salmon flies has never faded because of their beauty and complexity. I suppose I was initially drawn to salmon flies by what I see as the skill required to create them. Also, since so many of the flies are based on historical patterns, tying them is my way of participating in history. To a certain degree, I would rather live in the past than in the future. The past is reassuring. I know what happened in the past but not what will happen in the future. I am not the kind of person who will alter my life suddenly or pull up my roots and move on. I like to know what is going on around me and have some control.

My approach to tying is, I suppose, the same. The best fly I can produce is one I have thought out far in advance. I have an image of that fly in my mind's eye before I ever make the first wrap of thread. Once I plan my attack, that is the way I carry out the tying of the fly, with only occasional deviation or alteration. I like to think ahead and know that a particular thread wrap is going to a particular spot because it has a particular purpose. I am very critical about the placement of thread wraps and materials. Ninety percent of the wraps that go into a fly have already been planned when I start to tie. Everything is laid down for a reason, whether I am tying a soft hackle fly for trout or a feather-wing salmon fly.

LEFT: **_Quilled Eagle_**

Learning to tie Atlantic salmon flies is what made me start premeditating the process of tying a fly. A few years after I started to tie trout flies, I played around with what some might call Atlantic salmon flies, with the much-needed assistance of Joseph Bates's _Atlantic Salmon Flies & Fishing_. Because I had been tying custom-order trout flies since 1975 for Buz's Fly and Tackle in Visalia, I had developed generally good skills. To build on those skills, it seemed appropriate to apply my ability to something that I felt required more expertise. When the January 1977 issue of _Fly Fisherman_ came out with Poul Jorgensen's Orange Parson salmon fly on the cover, I was impressed. I had to tie it. It was the first legitimate full-dress fly I ever tied and one of the very few I still possess. To this day, I embarrass and humble myself occasionally by pulling it out and taking a look. Then, in 1978, Jorgensen's _Salmon Flies_ was published. I bought my copy on February 3, 1979, and immediately went to work, following the techniques in his book. Poul was the biggest initial influence in getting me seriously involved with salmon flies. I really appreciate his book, even with its flaws, and am convinced it was the catalyst that began the resurgence of tying and collecting feather-wing Atlantic salmon flies. Talk with any flytyer who has been tying salmon flies for five or ten years, and very likely Poul's book is what got them started.

Early on, a friend and fellow flytyer in my area, Dr. Gene Mathias, went to New Boston, New Hampshire, to take a class on Atlantic salmon flies with Bill Hunter. When Gene returned, he asked me to come over one evening so he could share some of the techniques he learned. I stayed that night until well after midnight, taking prodigious notes as he tied a Canadian Black Dose. I still have the six pages of notes carefully stored in the front of my copy of Jorgensen's book. One of the biggest benefits to my tying occurred when several local tyers, through Gene, invited Bill Hunter to California in 1982 to instruct a class. That class was a turning point in my tying. The most valuable technique to me was how to mount a married feather wing on a fly properly and consistently. To this day, the method I teach to students is Bill's. Gene was also helpful when I was starting out by providing encouragement, praise, and a constant supply of materials that I was unable to find elsewhere. He also put me in touch with Ron Alcott, who shared with me his research on materials and history. Without their early help and support, my tying would have progressed much more slowly, if at all.

As my flies evolved, I tied a number of better-known Atlantic salmon flies, but grew to prefer the more obscure patterns. There are many wonderful flies that people are unaware of. Although I rarely create flies—since there are more than enough for me to choose from—I do often improvise by contributing my own ideas and interpretations, as I did in the Nicholson, by changing an existing pattern to achieve certain combinations of colors and textures. I like my flies to be three-dimensional and may modify a fly to give it more substance. Adding horns to the George Kelson dressing for a Black Dog, for instance, better balances the dimension of the wing with the fullness of the heron throat. I have little problem justifying such a change in a fly, either historically or ethically.

Every experienced tyer has a distinct style. An aspect of my style is that I work at flytying in a very technical manner. I may not have the artistic eye that some people do, but I am very good with structure. If I were an artist, I would be a paint-by-number artist who would follow the lines precisely. Students like the technical approach because they want information that is cut and dried and that follows a specific direction. As students I have taught begin to develop, it is gratifying to see them leave my structured methods and blaze ahead into their own personal styles. Teaching is a great learning tool for me. When a student asks me why I do something, I have to know the answer. I cannot bluff my way through.

My emphasis on structure and technique appears to lead students to a more ready understanding of what I am trying to teach. Tyers who are more freethinking may have difficulty conveying to students why they do what they do. A student might pick up some tying tips but will not comprehend why the execution of the fly is accomplishing what it is meant to do. If I can impart a new understanding of technique, handling of materials, and thread control, I have accomplished my

OPPOSITE:

Nicholson

purpose. For every class, I have a standard introduction: After taking this class, if you never tie another Atlantic salmon fly again, my feelings will not be hurt because my purpose is to teach techniques that can apply to all facets of tying. That is why I like salmon flies. Tying them is an ongoing process of learning skills applicable to the whole spectrum of flytying.

Tying flies is a personal activity, a way of expressing myself. I would be lying, though, to say that I am not thrilled when someone walks into my tying room and is impressed with a fly I have tied. But that is not going to help or hinder me from getting better. My only goal is to get better in my own eyes, not to flaunt my work for other people. When I look at my flies, especially my Atlantic salmon flies, I see flaws. I try to educate myself to solve the problem that caused a flaw so that I might avoid making the same mistake again. Among the flytyers I know, the better they are, the more they are dissatisfied with their work. It is not that they think they are poor flytyers. They know they are good—and they don't have to be told they are good—but they know they are capable of more, and are constantly striving for it.

If I ever reach the point where I do not think I am capable of more, whether or not I actually am as good as I can be, I suppose I will quit. It is not due to a desire for perfection. I do not consider myself a perfectionist. Nor do I desire to reach perfection. What is perfection in an Atlantic salmon fly? It is only in the eyes of the beholder. I do consider myself a picky flytyer who likes things to be where I want them to be. Being critical of my flies keeps me tying. I would like to tie a good one some day. It seems odd—ridiculous—that some salmon fly tyers become so obsessed with their tying. At times, we take simple fur and feather far too seriously. The world is not going to turn on an Atlantic salmon fly. It is important to have a sense of humor about it.

For me, tying Atlantic salmon flies is an intense process, often taking four to a dozen hours to tie one fly. For relaxation, I escape with trout flies, or spin a hair bug, or play with a hair-wing salmon or steelhead fly. Possibly I will concoct a fly for a local stream. I also like taking on challenges. A few years ago, a friend showed me a headless fly by Ed Haas, the famous tyer of steelhead flies who lived in northern California. Shortly before Ed's death, I asked him about the fly. He told me it was a joke to a customer in Chicago. Ed's flies had

very distinct and consistent heads, but the customer preferred a fly with a very small head. Before Ed had a chance to tell me how he had made his headless fly, I contacted several friends around the United States, challenging them to come up with a solution. We ended up with six or seven good methods, and all of us learned by the experience. None were terribly practical in application but were a lot of fun to devise and share with each other—and not one of our methods for tying a headless fly was close to what Ed actually did. Before long, a new challenge appeared for us: tying a threadless fly.

It is important for me to be known as a versatile tyer. I am not fond of being labeled only as an Atlantic salmon fly tyer because I enjoy all types of tying and think I am competent and comfortable when tying almost any type. Years ago, Lefty Kreh told me that he felt Poul Jorgensen was the best tyer in the United States. I asked him why, and he responded, "Poul can tie any fly equally well." That struck me then and it does now. I have and always will want to tie all flies equally well, not to be like Poul, but as a matter of personal pride. I appreciate being known for the work I do with Atlantic salmon flies, but would equally appreciate recognition for tying a well-done size 28 Royal Wulff or a 4/0 saltwater streamer.

Most of my involvement with Atlantic salmon fly tying does not actually require my presence at the vise but entails communicating with other flytyers. A constant flow of mail arrives to and departs from my address. Thus far, the record number of letters I have sent in one day is fifteen. The record of receipts is an unknown, though if I do not get any mail on a particular day, I first assume that it is due to the death of my mail carrier or a similar tragedy. My telephone line is quite busy as well. I am not surprised as much by the sheer numbers of calls, as by the odd hours I receive them—from six in the morning my time to one or two in the morning the caller's time. The interest in salmon flies shown in my mail continues to expand at such a rate that keeping up with the correspondence is becoming more and more difficult.

The reason for all of the communication is that I like to put people in touch with one another. Perhaps I serve as a clearinghouse for salmon fly tyers. The phone calls, letters, and often lengthy audiotapes that I send and receive deal with almost every aspect of salmon fly tying one could think of. Sometimes people write me with questions. I like that. Many times I may not have an answer, but I probably know who does, and in finding the answer we all learn. Through the years, I have received numerous photographs, which are invaluable for watching a tyer's style develop as well as for sharing new techniques and approaches. Some write me about the history of the salmon fly and their interpretation of the writings of the early authors. Numerous packages appear, especially with materials to pass on to other tyers at more reasonable prices than can be found elsewhere. They are dispersed quickly—often to beginning salmon fly tyers.

The tyers I correspond with live in a fascinating variety of places. One would think that the hotbed for the tying of salmon flies would be the Northeast of the United States, and although I do receive a lot of correspondence from that area, I receive more, far more, from people in other parts of the country and hear fairly regularly from people in at least six other countries. Tying Atlantic salmon flies is certainly not a regional craft. My personal store of information is quite limited and would be more so if it weren't for all of my friends who share what they know with me. People know, or are surprised to find out, that I try to be a faithful writer, but I enjoy being a link in the chain that will help them and me.

JOHN VAN DERHOOF

LONG BEACH, CALIFORNIA

More than being intrigued by the beauty of Atlantic salmon flies, I am interested in creating a fly that is challenging, new, and different. Starting to tie salmon flies after tying most other flies is like going from a jigsaw puzzle with a hundred pieces to one with thousands. The most important rewards are the feelings of satisfaction and achievement and the desire to better oneself. The whole sport of fly-fishing, not only flytying, has done more for me than anyone can possibly imagine.

Many people are intimidated by fishing for Atlantic salmon and tying salmon flies. Fishing for Atlantic salmon will always be for a few because of the expense and exclusivity. Tying the flies, however, should not be held up in the stratosphere. If tyers get proficient at tying, there is no reason they shouldn't try Atlantic salmon flies. People are afraid they will be unable to afford the materials or to find the so-called authentic materials. That's not important. What is important is that someone can sit down and enjoy tying a salmon fly. If it means bustard must be simulated with three different colors and textures of brown turkey tail, that's fine. If tyers feel they need guidelines, they can use the fish as a means to set their standards. The fish are not concerned if a fly has authentic materials. And whether someone lives far from or close to Atlantic salmon fishing, learning to tie Atlantic salmon flies can always be viewed as a challenge.

I recommend that people learn from an accomplished

ABOVE:

Moonlight

tyer. Considering that I am self-taught, I am amazed that I have stayed with flytying so long. I learned to tie flies and to cast a fly rod and line over fifteen years of isolation, and only in the last eight to ten years have I been exposed to different people and their ideas. I had been spin-fishing for several years before I started to tie flies at the age of twelve. In 1963, I was watching the *American Sportsman* show on television and saw Lee Wulff tying flies with a bunch of kids. Thinking it looked easy, I immediately went to the garage and from the tackle box pulled out a couple of worm hooks. I stuck one in a carpenter's bench vise, got a spool of my mother's sewing thread and some feathers from the bottom of the parakeet cage, and started to tie a fly. My father walked in and saw what I was doing. That afternoon he took me to Ball and Frank's sporting goods in downtown Long Beach. The people at the tackle store started me out with some basic tools and materials, and within a year and a half I learned to tie standard dry flies using the *Noll Guide to Trout Flies*, and was supplying a few shops as a commercial tyer. For years I couldn't figure out how to do a whip finish, so I finished off the fly using rod-wrapping techniques.

Then, in the late 1960s, I became more adventuresome. The second book I bought was J. Edson Leonard's *Flies*. I tied the streamers and steelhead flies in the book. I even framed some of them. I still have a frame, not even fronted with glass, that displays steelhead flies I tied on short-shank hooks using

patterns designed by or promoted by the late Jim Pray. The Railbirds and Optics appealed to me because they were different. I dabbled with the salmon flies in Leonard's book and taught myself how to marry feather wings. Years later, after Poul Jorgensen's *Salmon Flies* came out, a friend gave it to me for Christmas. As soon as I looked at it, I knew I wanted to tie Atlantic salmon flies more seriously.

All flytyers start out as chameleons, then move on when they feel comfortable. The better they get, the less like chameleons they are. In the beginning, it was easy to be colored by the information in front of me. My first salmon flies looked tremendously like Poul Jorgensen's. Poul's book was an eye-opener for me. I taught myself to tie salmon flies from that book. I also learned a lot about materials and techniques and used it for patterns. Poul's book gave me great confidence. Until I looked at his photographs, I had never seen anyone tie an Atlantic salmon fly. The information he presented confirmed many of the methods I had picked up through trial and error, methods that applied to trout flies as well as salmon flies. More people have learned to tie salmon flies properly from Poul's book in the last thirteen years than they have from any other source. I occasionally hear dissenting remarks about his book, and they bother me, because whatever variations or inconsistencies it has, it is a landmark in the history of Atlantic salmon flies.

LEFT: *Gordon*

Having outgrown the chameleon in me, I now like to tie a salmon fly that is not a copy of a traditional pattern. Inventing a fly is a short process once I come up with an idea, and I have many ideas for flies. My mind is like a police computer that matches up certain features to create a facial impression. Onto this pictorial index of fly designs, I superimpose different materials. In the design process I follow, there is certainly some crossover between my flytying and my work as a landscape architect. I analyze an idea, try to actualize it, review and critique it, then revise what I have done and critique it again. What particularly carries over from my design background is the approach to color. I have a book that I use all the time, *Elements of Color*, by Johannes Itten, a Bauhaus instructor from the 1920s. I reread it often because color blendings, more than anything else, determine what I do in my flies. Texture is probably second, then form, since I can change form to a small degree halfway through tying the fly if I want to. Yet, when I have chosen a certain hook, I have pretty much picked my car and I am going to drive it all the way throughout the four to six hours it takes me to tie a fly.

Although most of my flies are tied to be framed, I have taken many of my culled flies—feather-wing flies that weren't up to snuff or experimental practice flies—and fished them for Pacific salmon, steelhead, and trout. Depending on the water conditions and the depth at which the fish are holding, I use a feather-wing fly fished subsurface or like a dry fly for steelhead. The glitter of the more translucent flies such as those with topping wings is much too bright when the flies are worked close to the surface, but when drifted in deep water, they seem to provoke a much stronger reaction from the fish. When a fly is fished with a taut line in heavy current, the materials condense close to the body and bounce up and down through the water, as if the fly is undulating. I have used Sir Richards, Jock Scotts, and Gordons, which are great in sizes 1/0, 2/0, 3/0, and even 5/0, and the fish have taken them.

Sometimes just for fun, I include fluorescent materials in a fly. I tie a traditional fly, say, a Green Highlander, with over-dyed fluorescent orange golden pheasant tippet as an underwing, fluorescent yellow and orange for the married wing, with a slash of turkey over that. The body is fluorescent with fluorescent hackles. One of these days, I want to find a method for marrying Krystal Flash, and I am working on a way to incorporate it into married wings.

Tradition in Atlantic salmon fly tying is not in the specific composition of a fly but in its general characteristics and qualities. A salmon fly has a basic style that identifies it as a salmon fly, and within this style, there are innumerable variations. A tyer does not have to follow a specific dressing to be right. It drives me nuts that someone will tie a fly according to a "traditional" pattern. What is "traditional"? There is no way of knowing. I can pick four books with four different patterns for a Jock Scott. There is no such thing as a traditional Jock Scott. Tradition died when the first Jock Scott was tied and fished, then stored away and lost forever.

To me, the tradition of the Atlantic salmon fly is meant to evolve. We would not have all the patterns we do today if tyers had not been experimenting in the late nineteenth and early twentieth centuries. Tradition would not have arrived here unless it had undergone changes—or it would have died long ago—and it will continue to carry on. We can fall back on it as a base, but let's not ride it until it sinks. Since flytyers on the west coast live far from where Atlantic salmon fly tying traditions were spawned, many want to be—perhaps have to be—a little different. So many people around the country are experimenting with this area of tying that it will inevitably expand in other directions. I feel that we need an insurgence of fresh thought, and perhaps some of the west coast crazies are among the catalysts who will start to inspire other generations of tyers to change styles and do things that are completely different.

With so many people tying and as the popularity of fly-fishing continues to grow, Atlantic salmon flies will enjoy a healthy future filled with expansion. The only problem is that in order to make a fly, any type of fly, a viable entity, it has to have the fishability to back it up. It is very hard to say what is or isn't fishable. If a plastic hula girl tied on a hook will catch a brown trout on the Madison River—and it has been recorded on film—then perhaps it is impossible to limit what can be construed as a fishing fly. Maybe the next great Atlantic salmon fly will be a plastic monkey that was dangling from last night's cocktail by its tail, then the next morning was tied onto a hook.

TED NIEMEYER

SEATTLE, WASHINGTON

I remember the excitement I felt as a young boy when I stepped in a stream with my first tied fly, cast it, and caught a fish. I was nervous, but I had a tremendous feeling of accomplishment about having just made this beautiful fly—which was actually not well constructed at all. As the trout came up and took that fly floating on the water, my heart was pounding. I hooked the fish and brought it in, but couldn't move my legs. They were frozen in pride, I suppose. There was a thrill that day the likes of which I have never had fishing again. Sitting down now to tie a fly is in a small part a re-creation of the experience of tying my first fly and catching my first fish on that fly. There is a sense of the unknown, a sense of expectation—a feeling that I am going to make the greatest fly or tie a fly better than anyone else can. Of course, I fail more often than I succeed.

Before I tied my first fly, I fished for trout and steelhead with eggs and worms and spinners on the Skagit, the Stillaquamish, and the Skykomish rivers not far from Seattle, where I grew up. My mother would leave our house at the north end of Lake Washington at daybreak to go to work, and soon after her departure I was on my bike to locate yet another secret trout hole, not to return until dark. One day a friend and I went up to the Skykomish River, quite a trip on a bike, to be sure. Late that afternoon we happened on a teenager with a stringer of eighteen- to twenty-inch trout, fresh and beautiful. We asked him what he had been catching the big trout on, and he told us that he fished with dry flies. He opened a plastic box filled with flies of radiant greens, yellows, reds, and oranges. He was not a good tyer as I recall, but his flies were as brilliant as a rainbow. Our eyes bugged. We couldn't believe he had caught all those trout on these beautiful flies. The seed had been planted.

On a Saturday morning, I caught the local bus with $1.35 in my pocket and went directly to Roy Patrick's house on Eastlake Avenue in Seattle, where he had a fly shop in his front room. I told Roy that I did not know how to tie flies but wanted to learn. For $1.15—leaving me enough money for bus fare home—he sold me a rickety old vise, some tying thread, and bags of very colorful feathers. The feathers turned out to be the floor sweepings from Herter's in Minnesota. All the colors of the rainbow had been gathered up and put into glassine envelopes, each of which cost twelve cents. I went home and started to tie the worst-looking flies. Yet they caught fish. That was it—that was the beginning.

As a teenager, I tied Atlantic salmon flies and fished them for steelhead. My grandad's sporting magazines occasionally had articles on east coast patterns for Atlantic salmon with illustrations of two or three flies. I copied them, tying the flies like wet flies for trout. My flies were crude but I caught a lot of steelhead. My grandad gave me an old three-part bamboo bait rod. I put a fly reel on it and cast the fly line through the bait guides. I was at an advantage in that my grandad was a boom boss who worked on Lake Washington for a lumber company. He had a master key to all of the locks on the gates of the logging roads, and we went fishing for steelhead on the smaller streams far into the mountains.

Years later, I moved to the east coast, where I met Charlie DeFeo, who became the biggest influence on my flytying. Charlie was among the people, including Keith Fulsher, Charlie Krom, and Everett Garrison, who frequented the Angler's Cove in New York in the 1960s. He was in his seventies when I met him, and after I got to know him a little, I took one of his flytying classes. I learned more from his lessons than I ever learned from anyone else. Charlie was a great man—a legend—but he was not an expert tyer. What was important was his supple touch in the handling of materials. His knowledge and experiences were vast. To me, he was a combination of all the books that had ever been written on flytying. Charlie and other people at the Angler's Cove kept asking me about what kind of flies I used. One day, I brought in a half-dozen dry flies and nymphs, all of which were exact imitations. Gladys Zwirz, who ran the shop, put the flies in the glass case near the front counter. Many people saw those flies, and I guess that's how my reputation began to grow.

Since I worked in Manhattan, I was able to take the time to browse the used bookstores. I found old books, including those by Ray Bergman, Reub Cross, J. Edson Leonard, and Art Flick. Early on, I decided to focus on North American authors, and in short order, I amassed a wonderful library. Some of the writing was not very good, but as I read the authors over and over, I started to piece together the history of flytying and fly-fishing. I always looked for information about materials. Very little was written about obtaining, handling, grooming, and protecting materials, and I realized that I had to learn on my own.

In late 1976, I was asked to take over the "Fly-Tier's Bench" column in *Fly Fisherman* magazine, which I continued to write until 1981. My main interest in the column was the people I studied. I always hoped that the flies I tied and the techniques I used reflected what I had learned from them. Through the column, I wanted to bring this information forward and share it with other tyers. If certain tyers were important to me, I thought they must be important to other people, too. So I tried to offer a little insight or a suggestion—for instance, to look at the wet flies of Helen Shaw, the dry flies of Walt Dette, or the steelhead flies of Syd Glasso. Few people in the East knew about Glasso when I first included him in a 1978 column. Many west coast readers wrote to thank me for mentioning the name. Later, I devoted an entire column to Glasso and also wrote columns on John Atherton, Ira Gruber, Lew Oatman, and Reub Cross.

Charlie DeFeo and I saw one another frequently. We often tied flies together, but most of the time we looked at flies and talked about patterns and materials. I would ask Charlie about nymphs, since that was one of my main interests. Although he had experimented with nymphs and had fished

for trout when he was younger, Atlantic salmon fishing was his first love. Charlie's observations about tying and fishing came from many years of experience. I remember that we discussed one of the great enigmas of flytying. Charlie told me that he could tie two dozen Atlantic salmon flies of the same pattern, using the same hook and the same materials, but only one would catch fish. Why? He didn't know. Nor did I. I have a fly of Charlie's that was passed among three fishermen in one day. Between them, they caught twelve salmon. With each fish they caught, the better the fly worked. When Charlie got it back at the end of the day, all that was left was a fraction of a black body, some loose yellow floss dragging behind the body, and a couple of fibers of hair. He said it was the finest fly he had ever tied. Others Charlie had used never produced like that one.

Charlie had been a commercial artist all his life and gave me a perspective on flytying from the artist's point of view. Through him, I learned about Preston Jennings's theories on color and fly design. Charlie showed me Jennings's Lady Iris and Lord Iris flies, and suggested that I study his methods for combining colors. Jennings's theories have to be read and reread to be understood thoroughly, but essentially he believed that fish saw the same insects differently under varying light conditions. The process he used to develop this theory of perception involved examining minnows and aquatic insects through a prism in varying levels of light. The natural insect, which is drab, acquires a brilliance when seen through the prism. The colors Jennings used in his flies represented the strong or weak light intensities under which the fish would be seeing the artificial fly. Although I do not subscribe to all of Jennings's theories, his ideas on color helped my tying immensely.

Charlie told me to go to an Atlantic salmon stream and turn over the rocks to see what was underneath. He was testing me. I did what he asked, and came back and told him that the New Brunswick rivers were full of stoneflies with yellow butts on their undersides. Why do you think, he asked me, that Atlantic salmon flies have yellow, green, or orange tags? He felt that the tag imitated the yellow band at the end of the stoneflies found in so many Atlantic salmon streams. He was right. Yet I have never found stoneflies in the stomachs of

OPPOSITE, CLOCKWISE
FROM TOP LEFT:

Nude Belle

Dark Belle

Light Belle

Midnight Belle

Belle

CENTER:

Black Belle

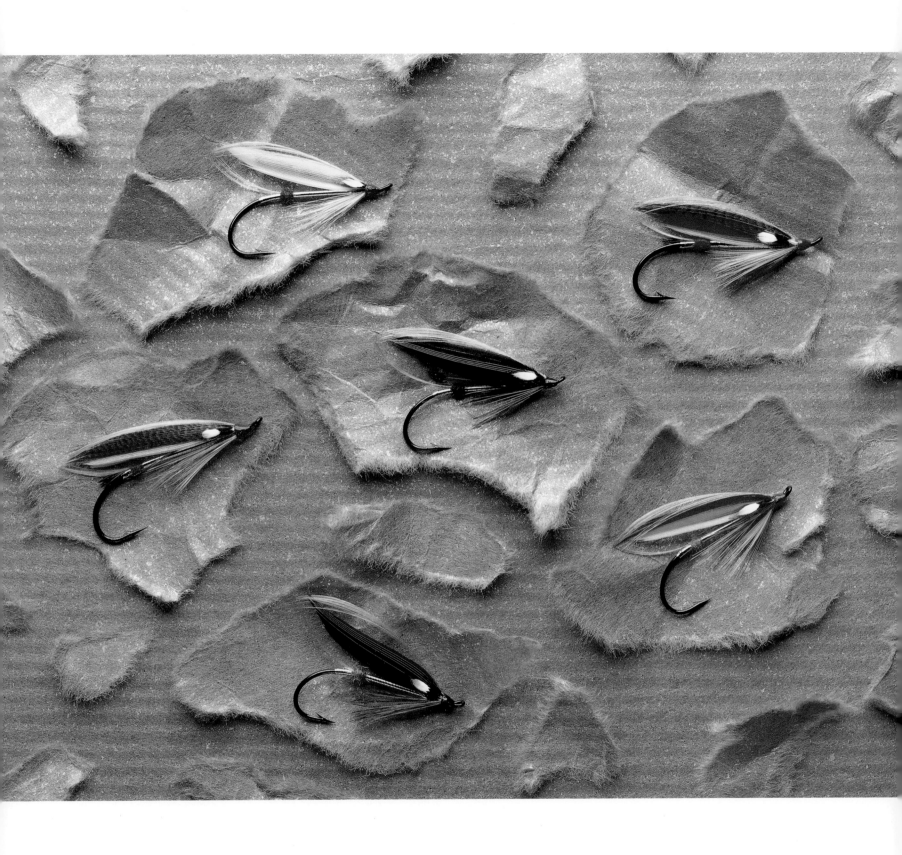

Atlantic salmon. Having theories about tying—that's part of the enjoyment and excitement for me.

Most tyers today make Atlantic salmon flies that are beautiful from the side, but they rarely turn the fly around to look down the eye. This is because salmon fly tyers seldom fish their flies enough to realize how they should perform in the water. Charlie taught me that a good fly enters the water properly, and to have proper entry a fly must have body. When a fly is cast, it should turn over, the leader should straighten, and the fly should settle and draw into the water head first, instead of flopping down on its side or on its tail. It should dive as a diver would and swim from the moment it hits the water. The ability of a fly to perform in this way is determined by the contours of the fly when it is viewed from the front. "What goes through the water the best?" Charlie once asked me. "A fish does. Look at a fish from the nose—that's the look you want in a fly." It was so simple. Charlie advised me not to tie an overly manicured Atlantic salmon fly that is straight up and down, like a painted razor blade.

Many Atlantic salmon fly tyers have gone beyond the basics of tying good fishing flies to exotic tying only for the sake of display. Although I admire their accomplishments, this is a step beyond the necessary purpose of flytying. If they want to be considered a flytyer's flytyer—among the best tyers working today—they should tie their flies to function as fishing tools. There never was or ever will be a valid reason to tie a fly except to deceive fish.

Because I fish the flies I tie and know what I want, I prefer to create my own Atlantic salmon and steelhead patterns rather than copy existing ones. When I was in the army, I did not have the time or resources to tie flies, but kept sketchbooks in which I drew flies. To this day, when I want to tie a new or unfamiliar fly, I never sit at the bench and launch into tying. I first make a pencil sketch, which tells me what I have to do when I ultimately begin to tie. I design a fly because I want to incorporate a new material or a new look, and in a sketch I can emphasize the area of the fly that has to be focused on to accommodate my desire. It may take four or five sketches, showing all sides of the fly, in order to achieve the effect I want. Then I tie the fly. Sometimes it works, and sometimes it doesn't.

Fish can certainly perceive the motion and profile of a fly. I am not convinced that fish can perceive color, but they can probably sense the relative intensity of color rather than specific hues. When I design flies like the Belle series, I enhance the color intensity by using contrasts. Therefore, if fish actually see color, my flies have an added advantage. Working with color gradations, I like to start with light tones on the bottom of the wing of a fly and progress to dark at the top. Designing the Belle flies so that they have motion in the water was also essential. The wing is haloed by the crest and tail, an effect that looks attractive and also has a function. The wing can move within the crest, and the fibers of the crest, being independent from the wing, can work like antennae in the water, imparting more action to the fly.

Like artists who study the work of the past, flytyers have always looked back and built on the achievements of the tyers before them. Contemporary tyers, however, often fail to devote as much time to the study of history and tradition as many of their predecessors did. The old guard had available much less reference material about the past than flytyers do today. Yet they studied every book they could get their hands on. Tyers today seem more interested in what is fashionable or what appears in the magazines. They want to be instantly accomplished in tying modern patterns rather than to take the time to learn from the past. Following the latest ideas is important, but tyers should also develop themselves by gathering all the insight they can from the tyers of the past. There is so much more to be learned, and I, for one, am still beginning to study.

M A R V I N   N O L T E

BAR NUNN, WYOMING

If I had to give up either flytying or fishing, the decision would not be difficult. I would give away all my fly rods and continue tying flies because it is so gratifying. When I tie a fly, I know I am going to have results when I am finished. When I fish, the feedback can be slim. Standing on a stream and casting a fly, watching the fly come down the current, casting the fly up and watching it come down again, is not as exciting as it is made out to be. Although I have always enjoyed fishing, I have never been a fanatical fisherman. It pales in significance compared with the tying.

For that reason, it doesn't bother me that I never fish the Atlantic salmon flies and some of the other flies I tie. That was my upbringing. I tied trout flies for three years before I fished with them and for seven years before I even saw another person tie a fly. In 1974, when I was living in Germany, my wife Victoria bought me a flytying kit because I was obviously in need of an activity outside

RIGHT: *Ballyshannon*

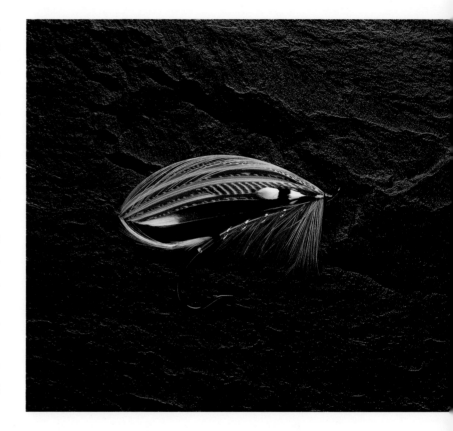

of my job. The only fishing I had done was with a spinning rod. I proceeded to learn how to tie from books. Through the mail, I obtained a Herter's catalog and ordered materials and, by chance, bought a copy of Poul Jorgensen's *Dressing Flies for Fresh and Salt Water*. I owe Poul Jorgensen a debt that he is unaware of and that I will never be able to repay. Persisting through his book, I tied nearly every fly in it—trout flies, bass bugs, saltwater flies—and, of course, the way I tie now is Jorgensen's style. After finishing his book, I ordered more books. The only trouble with learning from books is that you can ask them questions but they won't answer.

Flytying was immensely satisfying—with so many flies to tie, it was not boring—and gradually it replaced my other hobbies. I have always enjoyed working with my hands at activities that require a great deal of concentration. It was hard

to live in Europe and avoid taking up photography. I still have three or four camera bodies, a half-dozen lenses, and an equipped darkroom, though I no longer take photographs. I also whittled. I made my father a chess set and my daughter a teddy bear. I whittled plugs for fishing. I also whittled those chain links and balls in cages that you always see.

Making the chains was good training for tying flies, which involves a lot of conceptualization. Before you start to whittle, you have to look at the piece of wood and see the chain in there. After you whittle one chain, all you can do is keep making smaller and smaller chains. Flytying was easier and not as dangerous to my hands as whittling. At the time, I disarmed bombs for a living, which was a bit more dangerous

than whittling but excellent training for working with my hands. Although disarming bombs did not help my tying, it did teach me to focus with some intensity on what I was doing.

Two events radically changed my flytying. The first was studying insects. When I started tying trout flies, I really did not understand their basis in entomology. Because I followed a backward sequence—most people fish for trout before they tie flies—the connection didn't dawn on me until later in my flytying career that artificial flies were intended to imitate insects. In the back of my mind, I knew that was what I was supposed to be doing, but until I saw insects drifting down a trout stream and my fly floating among them, I did not realize the connection.

All my life I have been interested in nature. When I was young, I kept frogs in the vegetable crisper of the refrigerator. The low temperature caused them to go into hibernation, which meant they didn't need to be fed. When I took the frogs out, I would warm them up and feed them a couple of flies, and they would hop around. Then one day my grandmother opened the crisper to get a carrot and a frog croaked at her. That was the end of my frogs in the refrigerator. My father was in the army, and of all the places where we lived, my most vivid memory is of the Panama Canal Zone. Panama has huge insects. Across the street from our house was a primeval jungle with sloths, iguanas, banana treees, and insects—regulation insects. I wound up majoring in biology in college, but have only used my biology education in my flytying.

LEFT: *Dusty Miller*

When I finally watched other people tie flies, the importance of understanding insects struck me. I couldn't simply read about entomology. I had to collect the insects I was trying to imitate with my flies. My library became filled with books on aquatic entomology. Gary Borger's *Naturals,* one of my favorite books, prompted me build up a library of references. He is another person I owe a debt to. Among the flytying classes I teach now, I give one on entomology. I hand out little bottles of alcohol with insects in them. Each student has forceps to take out the bugs and a magnifying glass to study them. Studying insects may not have made me a better fisherman, but it vastly improved my tying. When you pick up a mayfly and look at how delicate it is, you start to tie much more sparse artificials. You wonder if it is necessary, because you caught that last trout on a Humpy,

which is not a spare fly.

The other event that dramatically affected my tying was learning about Atlantic salmon flies. First of all, I had to slow down and think about what I was doing, what would happen if I did something else, or did what I was doing incorrectly. As I tied more salmon flies, I could manipulate the materials rather than have the materials manipulate me. My esthetics changed. I am no longer satisfied with flies that have big, bulbous heads. They are good enough to catch a trout but they are unacceptable esthetically. My flies have got to be right. I tie a precise Wooly Worm. One of my favorite John Betts-isms is that you should tie a fly the way you want it to look. If you believe that a fly will work better after you fish it two or three times because it gets fuzzier, then you should tie it fuzzy to begin with.

The first Atlantic salmon flies I tied were from Jorgensen's early book. They were small fishing flies, very different from the salmon flies in his later book. I did not own a book on salmon flies until after I took a class in 1984 at the national conclave of the Federation of Fly Fishers, taught by Wayne Luallen, John Van Derhoof, and Dave McNeese. I could tell that salmon flies were difficult as well as challenging, but when I finished the class, I was not compelled to keep tying them. Only later did I become deeply interested in them. After moving to Wyoming, I started taking orders for flies. A customer requested a salmon fly. Tying salmon flies to order meant that I should know more, so I took the same class again the following year, with Wayne Luallen, John Van Derhoof, and Jim Carpenter. That was it. After that class, I stopped tying trout flies, except when my fly boxes got low, and tied only salmon flies.

After the second class, Wayne Luallen became my mentor. No one else has influenced my tying as much as he has, though our styles are radically different. I have learned a great deal about flytying on my own, but if I had to do it again, I would find someone to learn from. I wasted years. In 1981, when I finally saw a fly being tied, the tyer appeared to work so fast and meticulously that he seemed to have magic fingers. Being meticulous—that's something Wayne has taught me. He is the thinking tyer's tyer. For years I had been going through the motions of tying flies, never considering why a feather was doing what it was doing. By seeing how Wayne approached his own tying, I started to reflect on what I was doing and why. Wayne also critiqued my flies. No one else I have met will give an honest answer when asked an opinion. He is also extremely sharing of information and ideas. He won't just say, "That wing is ugly, Marvin." He has never told me that a fly has a problem and left it at that. He always recommends a certain technique that will make a fly come out better. I needed that, and his criticism has helped me immensely.

Meeting people is why the fly-fishing conclaves are so great. I attend the national conclave every year and spend most of my time watching tyers demonstrate and taking notes on what they do. When it is my turn to demonstrate, I like to tie old wet flies, small flies, size 8 and smaller, on pre-1905, blind-eye hooks with gut snells. I have spent considerable time analyzing the nuances of surgical gut, which is easier to find than silkworm gut. It behaves the same but is an unappealing yellow color. So I dye it, wax it, and polish it. I couldn't stop there. I had to develop a wax specifically for surgical gut. That epitomizes my approach. I would rather tie a fly made before World War I than the latest killer fly or my own invention. The period between the turn of the century and World War I, before eyed hooks and dry flies became popular, is the era that interests me. The old books on wet flies are enthralling and are not in as much demand as books on Atlantic salmon flies. The world has not discovered old wet flies, and since few people tie them, the books are available and reasonable in cost. That is my idea of creativity—going backward instead of forward.

Perhaps I have come full circle, because the first trout I caught, in 1977, was on an old English wet fly pattern, the Cow Dung, which imitates flies that hang around fresh meadow muffins. I'll remember that experience as long as I live. When I left Europe, I moved to New Mexico. Having just bought a fly rod and learned the rudiments of lobbing a fly, I went fishing for trout on the San Juan River. The water was clear. As I retrieved the fly to cast it again, this form came out of the depths, just as in a shark movie, chasing my fly. Had I not stared in wonderment at this animal emerging from the deep, I would have pulled the fly right out of its mouth. As it was, I forgot there was a fly at the end of my line. This little brown trout—which I remember as a foot long, so it must have been eight inches—came up and smacked that Cow Dung. I had the presence of mind to clip off the fly and save it. I thought everyone tied wet flies, but it turned out I was the only one with a Cow Dung in my box. I still fish with wet flies when they are snelled with monofilament.

Tying wet flies is very similar to tying Atlantic salmon flies in that it entails the quest for materials—golden plover, moorhen, and jackdaw feathers, water rat fur, fox ear. There are also some rather pedestrian feathers such as coot and snipe. Because few people tie old wet flies, land rail feathers are cheaper than bustard, which so many salmon fly tyers are trying to find. The word "bustard" does not flow off the tongue. Plover, moorhen—I like the sounds. Just a few tyers I know are curious about the old wet flies out of a sense of tradition and history. Handling the materials for wet flies is similar to handling the materials for Atlantic salmon flies because both have feather wings. It is easier, however, to put a wing on a big hook than on a small one. A salmon fly should be as sparse and tidy as possible. Sparse and tidy on a 3/0 hook for a salmon fly is different from sparse and tidy on a tiny hook for a wet fly. Also, the wet fly hooks come in wonderful odd sizes—sizes 3, 7, 15, 17. The whole area fascinates me. Perhaps I would be a better salmon fly tyer if I had started with those little wet flies, but I am definitely a better wet fly tyer now that I tie salmon flies. The skills are eminently transferable. All my flies look better since I started tying salmon flies.

I have only tied about two dozen different Atlantic salmon fly patterns—and have tied them over and over again. I like to get a fly right before moving on to another pattern. I am not very adventurous about creating flies, but consider myself adept at interpreting other people's patterns in my own style. I tell myself that if I get good, then maybe I will create a pattern. With Atlantic salmon flies, there is no end, no pinnacle, I will ever reach. I still feel the satisfaction that thrilled me when I started to tie flies. It is rewarding when someone looks at one of my salmon flies and says, "That's beautiful. How did you do that?"

ERIC OTZINGER

ENCINITAS, CALIFORNIA

Atlantic salmon flies are the pinnacle of flytying. Other flies, such as traditional streamers, are also difficult to tie, but tying salmon flies is a game of tensions, similar to building a house of cards. You see how much you can stack up and hope that it all doesn't collapse. People who tie salmon flies come up to me and complain, "I tied on the wing, but when I put that last topping over the wing, the whole thing fell apart." The skill is in controlling the tying thread as well as the materials, and as long as everything is just right, it will work.

After tying trout flies commercially for nine years and becoming quite proficient, I wanted to try the more challenging and colorful Atlantic salmon flies. At first I collected the materials for the sake of the materials, and went through a phase of researching information on the birds from which the feathers came and learning the Latin names for the various species. I was fascinated with these colorful feathers that came from faraway places in South America or Asia. I like exotic things—Tanzanian coffee, imported beer, traveling to unusual locations. I also love the textures of the materials—that's what it comes down to. A white hen feather can be dyed yellow, and it will work as well in a salmon fly as a toucan feather will. The only difference is the texture. A turkey feather can be painted with a pattern that will imitate speckled bustard, but the texture is not going to be quite the same. From handling and manipulating the mate-

ABOVE:
Niagara

rials, I really appreciate the texture of feathers, whereas someone less knowledgeable will look at a salmon fly and not see the difference between one feather and another.

When I first started tying trout flies in the 1970s, I knew very little about materials. I checked out some books from the library. One was the *The Art of the Wet Fly and the Flymph* by James Leisenring. I remember thinking, "This guy is crazy. He's talking about tying flies with raccoon fur and otter and hare's mask—and all of these bizarre furs and feathers. Where am I going to find this stuff?" I did manage to obtain some flytying materials from sports shops around Los Angeles and started tying basic patterns, but my initial efforts were crude. I had only been tying for a couple of months when my dad—the doting father—marched down to the local sporting goods store in Glendora and said to the proprietor, "Look what my son is tying. Aren't these great?" The proprietor said, "Yeah, I'll take four dozen of those." Immediately, at the age of fourteen, I became a commercial tyer. The fly was a Mosquito, and to this day I've tied more Mosquitos than any other fly.

An initial problem was that I had a seemingly huge order and no feathers to tie all these flies. The problem was resolved with a visit to Johnny's Sporting Goods in Pasadena, which carried a selection of flytying materials from Buz's Fly and Tackle in Visalia. Later I found out about Ned Grey's Sierra Tackle in Montrose. My father drove me there, and when I walked in, I saw that it was the dream store, with all the furs and feathers I had read about but had been unable to find. After I got my driver's license, I made many more enjoyable visits to Ned's. It was like a sanctuary from the rest of the world, with its friendly atmosphere and faint aroma of mothballs.

When I got more involved with Atlantic salmon flies, I came to feel that the more substitute materials utilized, the better. Fly-fishing is a somewhat hypocritical sport. Flytyers use feathers and furs from numerous animals, while expending great effort to preserve the fish and their habitat. I started to look for substitutes for my own tying and, after a year and a half, developed an alternative to Indian crow feathers. The most difficult part of developing the process was arriving at the correct tonalities. At first, I produced wild color casts, often without knowing how they occurred. Batches of feathers dyed two months ago still look slightly different from a batch made last week. The discrepancies can be justified because the actual Indian crow feathers vary from bird to bird. I have also worked on a method of duplicating speckled and florican bustard using dyes combined with a process related to photography. So far, the results have been inconsistent.

In my Atlantic salmon fly tying, I have learned more from other people than I have from books. The first time I met Wayne Luallen, in 1983, he gave me a lot of inspiration, as well as at least a dozen tips on how to improve my flies. As I met other tyers, my flies improved dramatically. I know the basic information about the development of the salmon fly, but rarely read about its history. I use the pictures and dressings of traditional flies in books as reference, and have chosen to develop my own style. When looking too much at what has been done in the past, one tends to copy that style. Some tyers examining my flies might say that they do not look like traditional salmon flies. This is because they incorporate subtle trademarks of my style that often result in a sleek and somewhat sparse tie.

Although I have created several original trout flies, I have only invented a couple of Atlantic salmon flies. One is called the Overkill because it is complicated, with an unconventional marrying of feathers. The other, the Bonanza, came about when I worked at a fly-fishing store. Customers coming into the store sometimes talked of being able to obtain materials for me, but usually were unable produce. One day, a man came in and told me he had a business raising macaws. I happened to mention that toucan feathers were also hard to find. He said he knew someone with frozen toucans that had died in transit from South America. To my surprise, he called me back a couple of days later and told me that he had the birds in his freezer for me. The toucan plumage provided such an array of pastel colors—yellows, oranges, reds, greens—that I decided to tie a fly using this subtle palette. Bonanza was the outcome.

I have tied some Atlantic salmon flies—always simplified feather-wing and hair-wing patterns—for people who want them for fishing. One customer was going to a lodge in Québec, where people were very status conscious. He wanted to fill his Wheatley boxes with a hundred traditional hairwings and feather-wings to impress the camp clientele. He took the flies with him but didn't fish them. He wound up using a fly that looked like a Glo Bug.

It is a curious fact that many people tie Atlantic salmon flies but do not use them for fishing. They are so beautiful that people enjoy tying them, yet are reluctant to fish them. I agree that tying Atlantic salmon flies is more of an art form, better suited for exhibition. Some Atlantic salmon fly tyers are very intense about their tying. The field has become so refined that the only people who can truly appreciate the complexity of these flies are the people tying them. Becoming the best tyer possible seemed important to me in the beginning, but tying creative patterns in my own style and experimenting with substitute materials are what I now enjoy the most.

OPPOSITE:

Bonanza

Appendix

Dressings

Bibliography

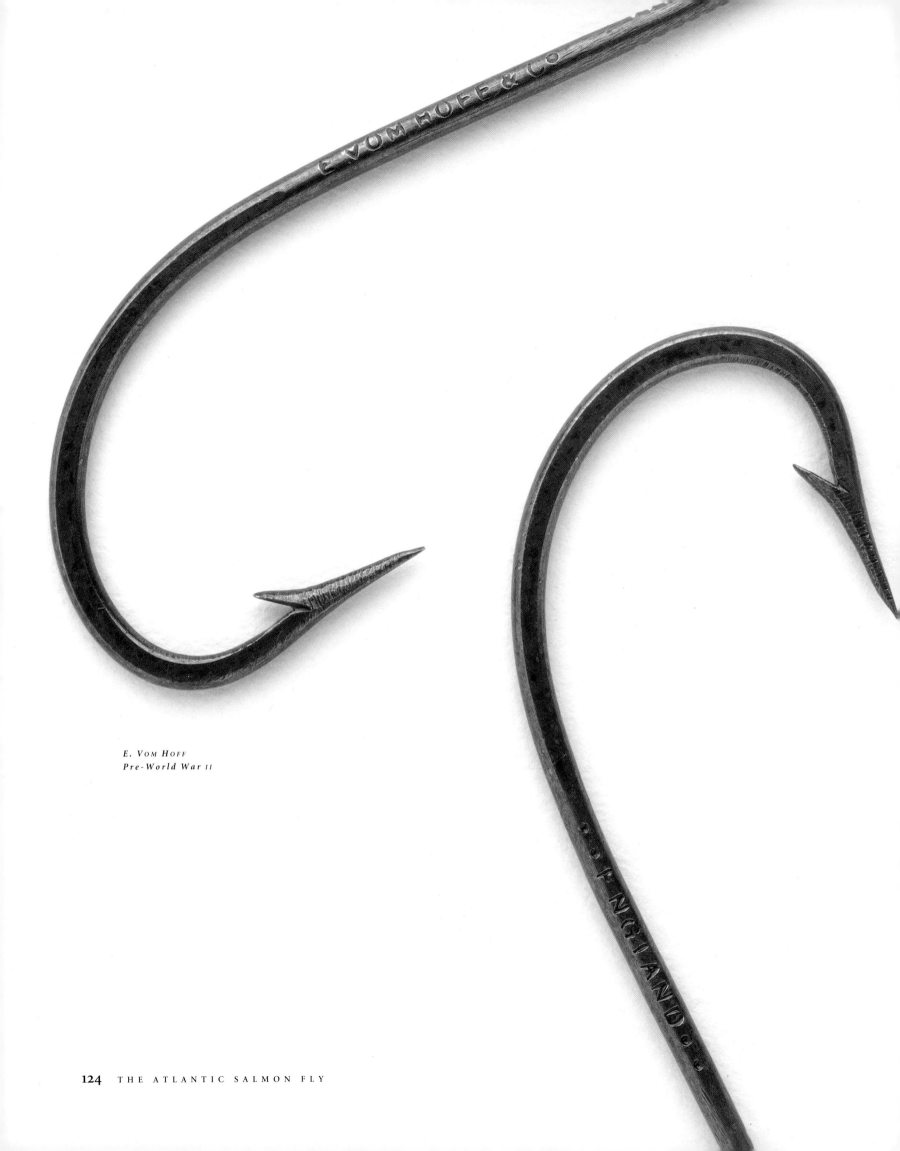

E. Vom Hoff
Pre-World War II

DRESSINGS

Ron Alcott

Colonel's Lady

HOOK Size 4/0 unknown British

TAG Extrafine oval gold tinsel

TAIL Golden pheasant crest and barred wood duck

BUTT Black ostrich herl

BODY Claret silk floss

RIB Flat gold tinsel and fine gold lace

HACKLE Claret neck hackle

THROAT Kenya crested guinea fowl

WINGS Lady Amherst pheasant tippets

SIDES Jungle cock

CHEEKS Blue chatterer

TOPPING Golden pheasant crest

HORNS Barbs of Lady Amherst pheasant center tail

HEAD Black

Jock Scott

HOOK Size 4/0 unknown British

TAG Extrafine oval silver tinsel and pale yellow floss

TAIL Golden pheasant crest and Indian crow

BUTT Black ostrich herl

BODY Rear half: golden yellow floss butted with black ostrich herl and veiled with toucan; front half: black floss

RIB Fine oval silver tinsel over the golden yellow floss, flat silver tinsel and silver lace over the black floss

HACKLE Black neck hackle over the black floss

THROAT Speckled guinea fowl

WINGS White-tipped turkey tail, married strips of peacock wing, yellow, scarlet, and blue swan, speckled bustard, florican bustard, and golden pheasant tail

WING VEILINGS Peacock sword feather, married strips of teal and barred wood duck, and strips of bronze mallard

SIDES Jungle cock

CHEEKS Kingfisher

TOPPING Golden pheasant crest

HORNS Blue and yellow macaw

HEAD Black

Megan Boyd

Blue Doctor

HOOK Size 1/0

TAG Silver twist and yellow silk

TAIL Golden pheasant crest and blue chatterer

BUTT Scarlet Berlin wool

BODY Light blue silk floss

RIB Oval silver tinsel

HACKLE Light blue

THROAT Blue speckled guinea fowl

WINGS Golden pheasant tippet in strands, speckled guinea fowl, golden pheasant tail, yellow, blue, and red swan, light mottled turkey, pintail, and mallard

TOPPING Golden pheasant crest

HORNS Blue and red macaw

HEAD Red lacquer band on black

Brora

HOOK Size 1/0

TAG Oval silver tinsel and lilac-pink silk floss

TAIL Golden pheasant crest and kingfisher

BODY Rear half: oval gold tinsel veiled with gold toucan; front half: black silk floss ribbed with oval silver tinsel

HACKLE Black heron

WINGS Cinnamon turkey, blue and white swan, and wood duck

HEAD Black

Childers

HOOK Size 3/0 low water

TAG Silver thread and pale blue floss

TAIL Golden pheasant crest and Indian crow

BUTT Black ostrich herl

BODY Rear half: golden yellow floss and yellow seal's fur; front half: ruby red seal's fur

RIB Flat silver tinsel and silver twist

HACKLE Lemon yellow badger

THROAT Golden pheasant breast feather and widgeon

WINGS Speckled bustard, blue, yellow, and red swan, peacock, orange swan, cinnamon turkey, and golden pheasant tail

CHEEKS Kingfisher

TOPPING Two golden pheasant crests

HORNS Blue and yellow macaw

HEAD Black

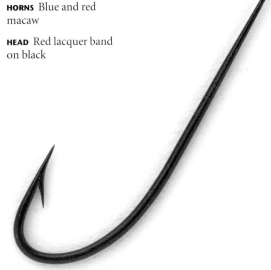

UNKNOWN
Late 1700s

Stewart Canham

Torrish

HOOK Size 5/0

TAG Silver twist and golden yellow floss

TAIL Golden pheasant crest and golden pheasant tippet in strands

BUTT Black ostrich herl

BODY Oval silver tinsel, butted with black ostrich herl, the rear two-fifths veiled with Indian crow

RIB Fine oval silver tinsel over the front three-fifths of body

HACKLE Lemon hackle with rib

THROAT Deep orange hackle

WINGS White-tipped turkey tail, yellow, red, and orange swan, florican bustard, golden pheasant tail, pintail, barred wood duck, and brown mallard

CHEEKS Jungle cock and Indian crow

TOPPING Golden pheasant crest

HORNS Blue and yellow macaw

HEAD Black

Dusty Miller

HOOK Size 4/0 unknown British

TAG Fine oval silver tinsel and golden yellow floss

TAIL Golden pheasant crest and Indian crow

BUTT Black ostrich herl

BODY Rear two-thirds: embossed silver tinsel; front one-third: orange floss

RIB Oval silver tinsel

HACKLE Golden olive hackle over the orange floss

THROAT Speckled guinea fowl

WINGS White-tipped turkey tail, married strands of teal, yellow, scarlet, and orange swan, speckled bustard, florican bustard, and golden pheasant tail, narrow strips of teal and barred wood duck, and narrow strips of brown mallard

SIDES Jungle cock

TOPPING Golden pheasant crest

HORNS Blue and yellow macaw

HEAD Black

Albert J. Cohen

Unnamed pattern from the 19th century

HOOK Size 5/0 Sunday, 1x-long

TAG Silver twist and violet floss

TAIL Golden pheasant crest, teal, golden pheasant tippet, and Indian crow

BUTT Black ostrich herl

BODY Black floss ribbed with oval silver tinsel, black ostrich herl at each joint, veiled with golden pheasant tippets

THROAT Orange saddle hackle and silver pheasant

WINGS Silver turkey tail, Lady Amherst pheasant, golden pheasant, speckled bustard, and violet, red, and blue goose, and bronze mallard

SIDES Jungle cock

CHEEKS Indian crow

TOPPING Golden pheasant crest

HORNS Red macaw

HEAD Black ostrich herl

Unnamed pattern from the 19th century
(front cover)

HOOK Size 6/0 Sunday, 1x-long

TAG Silver twist and yellow floss

TAIL Golden pheasant crest, red goose, and teal

BUTT Black ostrich herl

BODY Yellow, orange, ruby, and blue floss

RIB Flat silver tinsel and silver lace

HACKLE Red saddle

THROAT Blue saddle hackle

WINGS Underwing of yellow and red hackle and argus pheasant wing, outer wing of blue, yellow, and red goose, speckled bustard, and argus pheasant wing

SIDES Jungle cock and teal

CHEEKS Indian crow

TOPPING Golden pheasant crest

HORNS Red macaw

HEAD Black

Unnamed pattern from the 19th century

HOOK Size 7/0 Sunday, 1x-long

TAG Silver twist and golden yellow floss

TAIL Red goose and jungle cock

BUTT Peacock herl

BODY Golden yellow and black floss

RIB Silver lace

HACKLE Yellow

THROAT Black saddle hackle

WINGS Black hackle, white-tipped turkey tail, and yellow goose and brown spotted turkey tail

SIDES Jungle cock

TOPPING Golden pheasant crest

HORNS Red macaw

HEAD Black

ALEC JACKSON SPEYS
1984–90

Hans de Groot

The Macallan

HOOK Size 3/0 Partridge "Bartleet"

TAG Silver wire and scarlet floss

TAIL Golden pheasant crest (from an old, copper-colored bird) and orange tangara

BUTT Black ostrich herl

BODY Rear half: flat gold tinsel; front half: yellow, orange, and red seal's fur; body halves butted with black ostrich herl and orange tangara

RIB Oval silver tinsel

HACKLE Yellow hackle over the seal's fur, fronted with orange hackle

WINGS Underwing of speckled bustard flight feather, overwing of alternating married strips of speckled bustard and yellow and light orange swan

CHEEKS Agapornis tail feather and jungle cock

TOPPING Golden pheasant crest (from an old, copper-colored bird)

HORNS Blue and yellow macaw

HEAD Black

Royal Lochnagar

HOOK Size 3/0 Partridge "Bartleet"

TAG Silver wire and kingfisher blue floss

TAIL Golden pheasant crest and blue agapornis tail feather

BUTT Purple ostrich herl

BODY Rear half: flat silver tinsel; front half: purple seal's fur

RIB Oval silver tinsel

HACKLE Purple hackle over the purple seal's fur, fronted with vulturine guinea fowl

WINGS Underwing of vulturine guinea fowl breast hackle, overwing of alternating married strips of speckled bustard and kingfisher blue swan, with a wood duck veiling

CHEEKS Silver anhinga, jungle cock, and fairy blue bird

TOPPING Golden pheasant crest

HORNS Blue and yellow macaw

HEAD Black

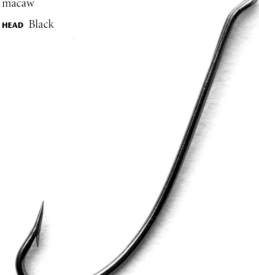

Jerry Doak

Black Dose

HOOK Size 2 single salmon

TAG Fine oval silver tinsel

BUTT Yellow silk floss

TAIL Golden pheasant crest

BODY Black wool

RIB Fine oval silver tinsel

HACKLE Palmered black cock neck hackle

WINGS Golden pheasant tippets, married strips of red, yellow, and blue goose shoulder, florican bustard, and mottled turkey, teal flank, and bronze mallard

CHEEKS Jungle cock

TOPPING Golden pheasant crest

HEAD Black

Copper Killer

HOOK Size 2 single salmon

TAG Fine oval gold tinsel and fluorescent green floss

TAIL Golden pheasant red breast fibers

BUTT Fluorescent red floss

BODY Flat copper tinsel

RIB Fine oval gold tinsel

THROAT Orange cock neck hackle

WING North American pine squirrel tail

HEAD Red

ALEC JACKSON SPEYS 1984–90

Oriole

HOOK Size 2 single salmon

TAG Fine oval gold tinsel

TAIL Golden pheasant red breast fibers

BODY Black wool

RIB Fine oval gold tinsel

THROAT Brown cock neck hackle

WING Golden pheasant red breast fibers and gray mallard flank dyed lemon yellow

HEAD Black

Rutledge Fly

HOOK Size 2 single salmon

TAG Fine oval silver tinsel

TAIL Fluorescent green floss

BODY Rear half: fluorescent green floss; front half: peacock herl

RIB Fine oval silver tinsel

THROAT Peacock sword fibers and black cock neck hackle

WING Black squirrel tail

HEAD Black

Warren Duncan

Buck Bug

HOOK Size 8 Tiemco 7999

TAG Extrafine oval silver tinsel

BUTT Fluorescent orange floss

BODY Mule deer hair

HACKLE Brown

HEAD Black cement

Copper Killer

HOOK Size 8 Partridge single salmon

TAG Extrafine oval copper tinsel and fluorescent green stretch nylon

TAIL Golden pheasant red body feather

BUTT Fluorescent red wool

BODY Flat copper tinsel

RIB Fine oval copper tinsel

HACKLE Hot orange

WING Fiery brown calf hair

HEAD Fluorescent red cement

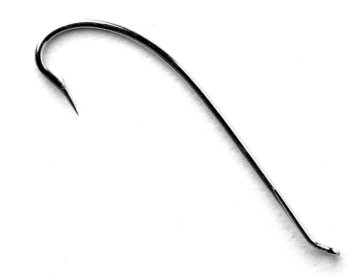

Steve Fernandez

Cosseboom

HOOK Size 8 Partridge single salmon

TAG Extrafine oval silver tinsel

TAIL Dark green floss

BODY Dark green floss

RIB Fine oval silver tinsel

WING Gray squirrel tail

HACKLE Yellow

HEAD Fluorescent red cement

Green Butt

HOOK Size 10 Partridge double Wilson and size 8 Tiemco 7999

TAG Extrafine oval silver tinsel

BUTT Fluorescent green stretch nylon

BODY Black floss

RIB Fine oval silver tinsel

HACKLE Black grizzly

WING Black bear hair

HEAD Black cement

Green Machine

HOOK Size 8 Tiemco 7999

TAG Extrafine oval silver tinsel

BUTT Fluorescent green stretch nylon and fiery red stretch nylon

BODY Green mule deer hair

RIB Brown neck hackle

HEAD Black cement

Hairy Mary

HOOK Size 8 Partridge single salmon

TAG Extrafine oval gold tinsel

TAIL Golden pheasant crest

BODY Black floss

RIB Fine oval gold tinsel

HACKLE Blue

WING Fiery brown calf hair

HEAD Black cement

Squirrel Tail

HOOK Size 8 Partridge single salmon and size 12 Partridge double Wilson

TAG Extrafine oval silver tinsel

BUTT Fluorescent red stretch nylon

BODY Black floss

RIB Fine oval silver tinsel

HACKLE Fiery brown

WING Pine squirrel tail

HEAD Black cement

Undertaker

HOOK Size 8 Partridge single salmon, size 8 Tiemco 7999, and size 12 Partridge double Wilson

TAG Extrafine oval gold tinsel

BUTT Green stretch nylon and fiery red stretch nylon

BODY Peacock herl

RIB Fine oval gold tinsel

HACKLE Black grizzly

WING Black bear hair

HEAD Black cement

Easy Off

HOOK Size 1/o Partridge "Bartleet," with modified bend, flattened eye angle, and barb removed, painted matte black with white splatters

TAIL Golden pheasant crest

TIP Black thread, lacquered

BODY Rear half: none; front half: sky blue floss with trace of royal blue floss dubbing

HACKLE Silver pheasant black body feather and silver pheasant zebra-striped body feather, palmered

THROAT Silver pheasant black body feather

WING Argus pheasant wing with short strips of bleached argus pheasant wing fibers married into cut openings

CHEEKS Jungle cock

HORNS Blue and red macaw, below hook shank

HEAD Black

Pompadour

HOOK Size 1/o Partridge "Bartleet," with modified bend, flattened eye angle, and barb removed, painted matte black

TIP Variegated embossed silver tinsel

TAG Yellow floss

TAIL Golden pheasant crest

BODY Rear five-sixths: tarnished embossed silver tinsel; front one-sixth: royal blue floss dubbing

THROAT Silver pheasant black body feather fibers

WING Florican bustard with three turkey tail fibers dyed silver-gray

CHEEKS Jungle cock

TOPPING Golden pheasant crest

HEAD Black

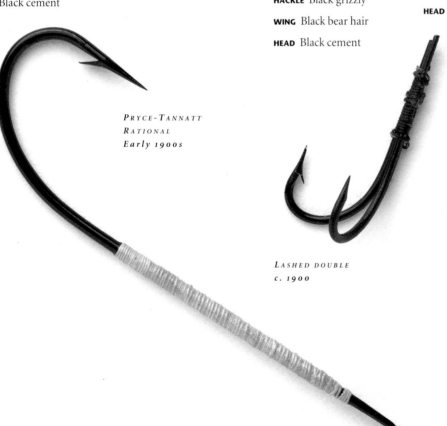

PRYCE-TANNATT RATIONAL Early 1900s

LASHED DOUBLE c. 1900

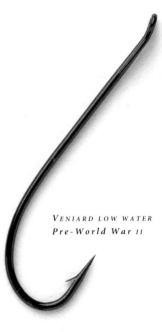

VENIARD LOW WATER Pre-World War II

Untitled

HOOK .032-inch piano wire, formed, filed, and painted matte off-white

TAIL Golden pheasant crest

BODY Mixed sky blue and fluorescent green floss dubbing over front one-fourth of shank

TIP Tail and palmer tie-down: white thread, lacquered

HACKLE Palmered goose shoulder, dyed silver-gray, stripped on one side, and every other fiber removed

THROAT Silver pheasant black body feather fibers

WING Twelve pairs bleached golden pheasant tippets

CHEEKS Jungle cock

TOPPING Two golden pheasant crests

HEAD Black

STEVE FERNANDEZ PIANO WIRE HOOK 1990

Keith Fulsher

Black Reynard

HOOK Size 6 Partridge single salmon

TAG Oval silver tinsel and black floss

TAIL Guinea hen fibers

BODY Black wool

RIB Oval silver tinsel

WING Red fox guard hair

COLLAR HACKLE Black

HEAD Black

Blue Reynard

HOOK Size 6 Partridge single salmon

TAG Oval silver tinsel and fluorescent blue floss

TAIL Guinea hen fibers

BODY Flat silver tinsel

RIB Oval gold tinsel

WING Red fox guard hair

COLLAR HACKLE Bright blue

HEAD Black

Green Reynard

HOOK Size 6 Partridge single salmon

TAG Oval gold tinsel and fluorescent green floss

TAIL Guinea hen fibers

BODY Flat gold tinsel

RIB Oval silver tinsel

WING Red fox guard hair

COLLAR HACKLE Bright green

HEAD Black

Orange Reynard

HOOK Size 6 Partridge single salmon

TAG Oval silver tinsel and fluorescent orange floss

TAIL Guinea hen fibers

BODY Flat silver tinsel

RIB Oval gold tinsel

WING Red fox guard hair

COLLAR HACKLE Bright orange

HEAD Black

Yellow Reynard

HOOK Size 6 Partridge single salmon

TAG Oval gold tinsel and fluorescent yellow floss

TAIL Guinea hen fibers

BODY Flat gold tinsel

RIB Oval silver tinsel

WING Red fox guard hair

COLLAR HACKLE Bright yellow

HEAD Black

STEVE FERNANDEZ ALTERED PARTRIDGE "BARTLEET" 1990

Bill Hunter

Black Doctor

HOOK Size 2/0 Partridge low water, reshaped

TAG Fine oval silver tinsel and golden yellow floss

TAIL Golden pheasant crest and red ringneck pheasant collar feather

BUTT Red wool

BODY Black floss

RIB Medium-fine oval silver tinsel

HACKLE Bright claret neck hackle

THROAT Speckled guinea fowl body feather

UNDERWING Strands of golden pheasant tippet and strips of golden pheasant tail

LOWER WING Married strips of red, blue, and yellow goose shoulder

UPPER WING Married strips of peacock wing, light mottled turkey tail, and dark mottled turkey tail, with a bronze mallard roof

WING VEILING Married strips of barred wood duck and falcated teal flank

TOPPING Golden pheasant crest

HEAD Red

Green Highlander

HOOK Size 2/0 Partridge low water, reshaped

TAG Fine oval silver tinsel and golden yellow floss

TAIL Golden pheasant crest and barred wood duck

BUTT Black ostrich herl

BODY Rear one-fourth: lemon yellow floss; front three-fourths: bright green mohair

RIB Medium-fine oval silver tinsel

HACKLE Bright green Chinese neck hackle over the bright green mohair

THROAT Yellow Schlappen hackle

UNDERWING Golden pheasant tippets

LOWER WING Married strips of yellow, orange, and green goose shoulder

UPPER WING Married strips of peacock wing quill, mottled turkey tail, and golden pheasant tail, with a bronze mallard roof

WING VEILING Married strips of barred wood duck and falcated teal flank

SIDES Jungle cock

TOPPING Golden pheasant crest

HEAD Black

STEVE FERNANDEZ PIANO WIRE HOOK 1990

Poul Jorgensen

Charlie Krom

Jock Scott

HOOK Size 2/0 Partridge low water, reshaped

TAG Fine oval silver tinsel and golden yellow floss

TAIL Golden pheasant tail and red ringneck pheasant collar feather

BUTT Black ostrich herl

BODY Rear half: deep yellow floss veiled with yellow hen hackle; front half: black floss and black neck hackle; body halves butted with black ostrich herl

RIB Rear half: extrafine oval silver tinsel; front half: fine flat silver tinsel and fine oval silver tinsel

THROAT Spotted guinea fowl body feather

UNDERWING White-tipped turkey tail and peacock sword fibers

LOWER WING Married strips of peacock wing and yellow, red, and blue goose shoulder

UPPER WING Married strips of dark mottled turkey tail, light mottled turkey tail, and golden pheasant tail, with a bronze mallard roof

WING VEILING Married strips of barred wood duck and falcated teal flank

SIDES Jungle cock and kingfisher

TOPPING Golden pheasant crest

HEAD Black

Blue Rat

HOOK Size 1/0 Partridge single salmon

TAG Fine oval gold tinsel

TAIL Peacock sword fibers

BODY Rear half: Silver Doctor blue floss veiled with a length of blue floss; front half: peacock herl

RIB Oval gold tinsel

HACKLE Small bunch of grizzly hackle fibers tied over wing, with similar bunch tied in as a throat

WING Gray fox guard hair

CHEEKS Jungle cock and kingfisher

HEAD Red

Durham Ranger

HOOK Size 7/0 Partridge single salmon

TAG Oval silver tinsel and yellow floss

TAIL Golden pheasant crest and Indian crow

BUTT Black ostrich herl

BODY Equal sections of yellow floss, and orange, fiery brown, and black seal's fur

RIB Flat silver tinsel and silver twist

HACKLE Yellow badger

THROAT Light blue hackle

WINGS Jungle cock veiled with golden pheasant tippets

SIDES Jungle cock

CHEEKS Blue chatterer

TOPPING Golden pheasant crest

HORNS Blue and yellow macaw

HEAD Black

RAY BERGMAN DRY FLY c. 1950

Sir Conrad

HOOK Size 3/0 Partridge single salmon

TAG Fine oval silver tinsel and yellow floss

TAIL Golden pheasant crest and golden pheasant tippet in strands

BUTT Black ostrich herl

BODY Four equal sections: yellow floss, and burnt orange, fiery brown, and black seal's fur

RIB Flat silver tinsel and gold lace

HACKLE Burnt orange

THROAT Speckled guinea fowl

UNDERWING Soft black bear hair

WINGS Married strands of orange, yellow, red, yellow, and blue swan, florican bustard, and speckled bustard; narrow strip of speckled bustard married to broad strip of black-barred wood duck

CHEEKS Kingfisher

TOPPING Golden pheasant crest

HORNS Orange macaw

HEAD Black

UNKNOWN 1930s–40s

Blue Doctor

HOOK Size 1/0 Veniard low water

TAG Flat silver Mylar and yellow floss

TAIL Golden pheasant crest and strands of golden pheasant tippet

BUTT Fluorescent red tying thread

BODY Pearlescent Mylar piping dyed blue

THROAT Blue guinea hen breast feather

WING Gray squirrel tail

HEAD Red

Copper Killer

HOOK Size 4 Veniard standard salmon

TAG Flat silver Mylar dyed orange and fluorescent green floss

TAIL Partridge body feather

BUTT Fluorescent red tying thread

BODY Silver Mylar piping dyed orange

THROAT Orange hackle

WING Red squirrel tail

HEAD Red

Gold Fever

HOOK Size 4 Veniard low water

TAG Flat gold Mylar and yellow floss

TAIL Black hackle fibers

BUTT Black tying thread

BODY Gold Mylar piping

THROAT Guinea hen body feather

WING Gray squirrel tail over yellow-dyed gray squirrel tail

HEAD Black

Helmsdale Doctor

HOOK Size 2 Veniard standard salmon

TAG Flat silver Mylar and yellow floss

TAIL Golden pheasant crest

BUTT Fluorescent red tying thread

BODY Silver Mylar piping

THROAT Yellow hackle

WING Gray squirrel tail over fluorescent deep red floss

HEAD Black with a red band

Silver Monkey

HOOK Size 4 Veniard standard salmon

TAG Flat silver Mylar and fluorescent red floss

TAIL Golden pheasant crest

BUTT Black tying thread

BODY Silver Mylar piping

THROAT Grizzly hen hackle

WING Silver monkey over fluorescent green floss

HEAD Black

UNKNOWN 1850

Judy Lehmberg

Evening Star

HOOK Size 1½ Alec Jackson gold Spey

TAG Fine oval silver tinsel and red silk floss

TAIL Golden pheasant crest and barred wood duck

BUTT Black ostrich herl

BODY Rear three-fourths: fine oval silver tinsel and jungle cock, butted with black ostrich herl; front one-fourth: dark blue silk floss ribbed with fine oval silver tinsel

THROAT Jungle cock

WINGS Lady Amherst pheasant tippets

SIDES Barred wood duck

CHEEKS Indian crow

TOPPING Golden pheasant crest

HORNS Red macaw

HEAD Black ostrich herl and black thread

Wayne Luallen

Nicholson

HOOK 7/0 Sunday

TAG Silver twist

TAIL Golden pheasant crest, goose dyed scarlet ibis, and wood duck

BUTT European jay and black ostrich herl

BODY Three sections: scarlet and black silk floss butted with European jay and black ostrich herl; lemon and scarlet silk floss butted with scarlet hackle and black ostrich herl; orange and medium blue silk floss butted with medium blue hackle and dark orange coch y bondu hackle

RIB Flat silver tinsel and fine oval silver tinsel

THROAT Heron dyed black

WINGS Golden pheasant sword enveloped by jungle cock; speckled bustard, argus pheasant, light turkey, lavender, yellow, and scarlet turkey tail, and peacock herl

SIDES Pintail and jungle cock

TOPPING Golden pheasant crest

HORNS Red macaw

HEAD Black

Quilled Eagle

HOOK 3/0 Sunday

TAG Silver twist and peacock tail covert quill dyed yellow

TAIL Golden pheasant crest, peacock sword, speckled bustard, and goose dyed scarlet ibis

BUTT Black ostrich herl

BODY Peacock tail covert quill dyed yellow, with orange seal's fur at throat

RIB Oval silver tinsel

HACKLE Grayish tan maraboulike rump feather from buff ringneck pheasant

THROAT Spotted guinea fowl

WINGS Golden pheasant tippets veiled with jungle cock, and married strands of scarlet turkey tail and speckled bustard

SIDES Jungle cock

TOPPING Golden pheasant crest

HEAD Black

Mike Martinek

Mike's Red Ghost Special

HOOK Size 4 Partridge "Carrie Stevens"

TAG Medium flat silver tinsel

BODY Scarlet silk floss

RIB Medium flat silver tinsel

OVERBODY Red bucktail and golden pheasant crest

THROAT White hackle

UNDERWING Bronze peacock herl and golden pheasant crest

WING Scarlet hackle and dark gray-blue hackle

SHOULDERS Finely barred silver pheasant flank

CHEEKS Jungle cock

HEAD Black

Royal Marine

HOOK Size 4 Partridge "Carrie Stevens"

TAG Fluorescent orange thread, lacquered

BODY Flat silver tinsel and pearl transparent Mylar

OVERBODY Red bucktail and white bucktail

THROAT White hackle

UNDERWING Peacock herl and red golden pheasant crest

WING White hackle, purple grizzly hackle, and vulturine guinea fowl

UPPER THROAT Red hackle

CHEEKS Jungle cock

HEAD Black

Ted Niemeyer

Belle

HOOK Size 4 low water

TAG Medium flat silver tinsel

TAIL Golden pheasant crest and hot orange Lady Amherst pheasant tippet fibers

BUTT Hot orange wool

BODY Medium flat silver tinsel

THROAT Yellow and red hackle

WING Hot orange Lady Amherst pheasant tippet fibers as underwing; yellow, orange, red, and Silver Doctor blue swan under a sheath of bronze mallard

CHEEKS Jungle cock

TOPPING Golden pheasant crest

HEAD Hot orange

Black Belle

HOOK Size 6 low water

TAG Medium flat gold tinsel

TAIL Golden pheasant crest

BUTT Black wool

BODY Medium flat gold tinsel

THROAT Black hackle

WING Hot orange Lady Amherst pheasant tippet as underwing; black swan with four fibers of blue macaw married in

CHEEKS Jungle cock

TOPPING Golden pheasant crest

HEAD Black

UNKNOWN LOW WATER c. 1930

UNKNOWN Early 1900s

Dark Belle

HOOK Size 6 low water

TAG Medium flat silver tinsel

TAIL Golden pheasant crest and hot orange Lady Amherst pheasant tippet fibers

BUTT Hot orange wool

BODY Medium flat silver tinsel

THROAT Lemon and violet hackle

WING Hot orange Lady Amherst pheasant tippet fibers as underwing; yellow, orange, red, and Silver Doctor blue swan under a sheath of bronze mallard

CHEEKS Jungle cock

TOPPING Golden pheasant crest

HEAD Hot orange

Light Belle

HOOK Size 6 low water

TAG Medium flat silver tinsel

TAIL Golden pheasant crest

BUTT Light orange and flesh-colored wool, mixed

BODY Medium flat silver tinsel

THROAT Yellow and hot orange hackle

WING Yellow, orange, and red swan

CHEEKS Jungle cock

TOPPING Golden pheasant crest

HEAD Hot orange

Midnight Belle

HOOK Size 6 low water

TAG Fine flat light chartreuse tinsel

TAIL Golden pheasant crest

BUTT Hot pink wool

BODY Fine flat light chartreuse tinsel

THROAT Hot pink and black hackle

WING Hot orange Lady Amherst pheasant tippet as underwing; black and red swan with five fibers of blue macaw married in

CHEEKS Jungle cock

TOPPING Golden pheasant crest

HEAD Black

Nude Belle

HOOK Size 6 low water

TAG Medium flat silver tinsel

TAIL Golden pheasant crest

BUTT Hot pink and red wool, mixed

BODY Medium flat silver tinsel

THROAT Cream hackle

WING Hot orange Lady Amherst pheasant tippet as underwing, sheathed in cream and yellow swan

CHEEKS Jungle cock

TOPPING Golden pheasant crest

HEAD Hot orange

Marvin Nolte

Ballyshannon

HOOK Size 1/o Partridge "Bartleet"

TAG Silver twist and blue floss

TAIL Golden pheasant crest and Indian crow

BUTT Black ostrich herl

BODY Hot orange floss

RIB Broad oval silver tinsel

HACKLE Magenta saddle

THROAT Blue saddle hackle

WINGS White-tipped turkey tail, speckled bustard, argus pheasant, red, yellow, and blue turkey, and bronze mallard

SIDES Pintail

CHEEKS Jungle cock

TOPPING Golden pheasant crest

HEAD Black

Dusty Miller

HOOK Size 1/o Partridge "Bartleet"

TAG Silver twist and apple green floss

TAIL Golden pheasant crest

BUTT Black ostrich herl

BODY Embossed silver tinsel

RIB Broad oval gold tinsel

THROAT Olive saddle hackle and spotted guinea fowl

WINGS Golden pheasant tail, and green and claret turkey

SIDES Teal

CHEEKS Jungle cock

TOPPING Golden pheasant crest

HEAD Black

Eric Otzinger

Bonanza

HOOK Size 1/o Partridge "Bartleet"

TAG Copper wire and violet floss

TAIL Black golden pheasant crest and pale orange toucan

BUTT Black ostrich herl

BODY Pink floss ribbed with flat copper tinsel and oval silver tinsel

HACKLE Heron

THROAT Violet heron and salmon toucan

WING Emu hackle and yellow toucan

CHEEKS Blue chatterer

TOPPING Orange toucan and black golden pheasant crest

HORNS Hyacinth macaw

HEAD Copper tinsel and black thread

Niagara

HOOK Size 1/o Partridge "Bartleet"

TAG Gold wire and black floss

TAIL Lady Amherst pheasant

BUTT Black ostrich herl

BODY Four equal sections: yellow floss butted with yellow hackle; pea green floss butted with pea green hackle; red floss butted with red hackle; dark blue floss

RIB Fine oval gold tinsel over the first three sections, fine oval silver tinsel over the dark blue floss

THROAT Orange toucan and black heron

UNDERWING Black saddle hackle

WINGS Mixed mottled turkey tail, speckled bustard, and peacock wing

SIDES Wood duck and teal

TOPPING Golden pheasant crest

HORNS Red macaw

HEAD Red

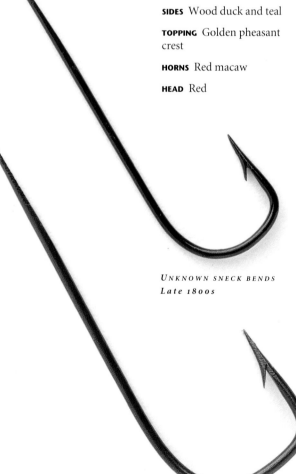

*UNKNOWN SNECK BENDS
Late 1800s*

Ken Sawada

Daybreak

HOOK Size 8/o Partridge, reshaped

TAG Silver wire and yellow floss

TAIL Golden pheasant crest, Indian crow, and blue chatterer

BUTT Dark blue ostrich herl

BODY Rear half: dark blue floss ribbed with medium oval gold tinsel, butted with dark blue ostrich herl, and veiled with toucan; front half: dark blue floss ribbed with broad embossed gold tinsel and oval silver tinsel

HACKLE Dark blue hackle on the front half of body

THROAT Bright orange hackle and blue peacock breast feather

WINGS Strips of yellow, light orange, dark orange, scarlet, crimson, and claret bustard, married with strips of light blue, dark blue, and lavender bustard, to make gradations from bottom to top

CHEEKS Indian crow

TOPPING Golden pheasant crest

HORNS Scarlet macaw

HEAD Black

Un-Married Angel

HOOK Size 8/o Partridge, reshaped

TAG Silver wire and yellow and lilac floss

TAIL Golden pheasant crest and mixed strips of blue macaw, yellow macaw, and pea green parrot

BUTT Pale blue ostrich herl

BODY Rear half: yellow floss ribbed with lavender floss and fine oval silver tinsel, butted with pale blue ostrich herl, and veiled with toucan; front half: lavender floss ribbed with orange floss and fine oval silver tinsel

THROAT Light blue heron and golden pheasant crest

WINGS Six golden pheasant crests, single strands of blue macaw, scarlet macaw, and Lady Amherst pheasant tail, and two strands of lilac bustard inserted between each crest

CHEEKS Blue chatterer

HORNS Scarlet macaw

HEAD Black

Paul Schmookler

(Tyer declines to list dressings.)

John Van Derhoof

Gordon

HOOK Size 5/o Mustad worm, reshaped to match 5/o Allcock blind eye

TAG Flat silver tinsel

TAIL Golden pheasant crest and Indian crow

BUTT Black ostrich herl

BODY Rear half: light orange floss and scarlet floss; front half: crimson seal's fur

RIB Flat silver tinsel and fine silver lace

HACKLE Dark claret heron over the crimson seal's fur

THROAT Light blue silver pheasant

UNDERWING Golden pheasant tippets, scarlet hackle, and peacock herl

WINGS Married strands of orange, burnt orange, crimson, scarlet, claret, and medium blue turkey, Lady Amherst pheasant, golden pheasant tail, and speckled bustard

SIDES Married strands of scarlet, orange, and medium blue turkey

CHEEKS Golden pheasant tippet and jungle cock

HORNS Blue and yellow macaw

HEAD Black with extrafine oval gold tinsel

Moonlight

HOOK Size 4/o antique Dee

TAG Flat silver tinsel

TAIL Golden pheasant crest and jungle cock

BUTT Black ostrich herl

BODY Rear half: flat silver tinsel veiled with kingfisher, butted with black ostrich herl; front half: black floss

RIB Rear half: extrafine oval silver tinsel; front half: wide flat silver tinsel, medium blue floss, and medium silver tinsel

HACKLE Black heron over the black floss

THROAT Light blue silver pheasant and guinea fowl

WINGS Married strands of cinnamon turkey, pale blue, medium blue, dark blue, and violet turkey, and speckled bustard, veiled with kingfisher

HEAD Black with extrafine oval gold tinsel

Bob Veverka

Double Ackroyd
(back cover)

HOOK Size 5/o antique

TAG Flat silver tinsel

TAIL Golden pheasant crest and golden pheasant tippet

BODY Alternating sections of yellow seal's fur ribbed with embossed silver tinsel and black floss ribbed with flat silver tinsel, butted after the first two sections with jungle cock

HACKLE Black Spey feather over the black floss and yellow hackle over the yellow seal's fur

THROAT Teal

WINGS Goose quill

CHEEKS Jungle cock

HEAD Black

Gardner
(back cover)

HOOK Size 3/o Sunday long Dee

TAG Oval gold tinsel and scarlet floss

TAIL Golden pheasant crest and golden pheasant tippet

BODY Yellow, green, and blue seal's fur

RIB Oval silver tinsel and flat silver tinsel

HACKLE Orange hackle from second turn of tinsel

THROAT Black Spey feather

WINGS Argus pheasant

CHEEKS Jungle cock

HEAD Black

HARRISON-BARTLEET
Late 1800s

PARTRIDGE "BARTLEET"
1990

UNKNOWN
Late 1700s

Jimmy Younger

Ghost
(back cover)

HOOK Size 2/0 low-water Partridge, eye removed

TAG Oval silver tinsel

TAIL European jay

BUTT Black ostrich herl

BODY Rear half: black floss; front half: black ostrich herl; body halves butted with flat silver tinsel and golden pheasant crest

HACKLE Black Spey feather over the black ostrich herl

WING Bronze mallard

HORNS Blue and yellow macaw

HEAD Black

Purple Ghost
(back cover)

HOOK Size 2/0 antique long Dee

TAG Oval silver tinsel

TAIL European jay

BUTT Black ostrich herl

BODY Rear half: purple floss veiled with golden pheasant crest; front half: black ostrich herl

HACKLE Purple and black Spey feather over the black ostrich herl

THROAT Guinea fowl

WINGS Purple goose quill

HEAD Black

WILSON UP-EYE
Pre-World War II

Three-Eyed Monster

HOOK Size 7/0 Sunday

TAG Oval silver tinsel and scarlet floss

TAIL Golden pheasant crest and Indian crow

BUTT Black ostrich herl

BODY Rear half: flat copper tinsel ribbed with oval silver tinsel, veiled with toucan, and butted with black ostrich herl; front half: purple floss ribbed with oval silver and fine flat copper tinsel

HACKLE Red hackle over the front half of body

THROAT Black hackle

WING Gray peacock pheasant

CHEEKS Red roller and palawan peacock pheasant

TOPPING Golden pheasant crest

HORNS Red macaw

HEAD Black ostrich herl

Tri-Color Spey

HOOK Size 3/0 Sunday long Dee

TAG Flat silver tinsel

TAIL Golden pheasant crest and tip of a golden pheasant breast feather

BODY Pale yellow, light blue, and scarlet seal's fur

RIB Flat silver tinsel and silver twist

HACKLE Gray Spey feather from third turn of tinsel

THROAT Teal

WINGS Argus pheasant

CHEEKS Jungle cock

HEAD Black

Arndilly Fancy

HOOK Size 6 Partridge double low water

TAG Fine oval silver tinsel

TAIL Golden pheasant crest

BODY Pale yellow floss

RIB Fine oval silver tinsel

THROAT Bright blue hackle

WING Black squirrel tail

CHEEKS Jungle cock

HEAD Red and black

Black Doctor

HOOK Size 6 Partridge double low water

TAG Fine oval silver tinsel

TAIL Golden pheasant crest and blue hackle tip

BUTT Red floss

BODY Black floss

RIB Fine oval silver tinsel

THROAT Natural guinea fowl

WING Dark brown squirrel tail

CHEEKS Jungle cock

HEAD Red

Dusty Miller

HOOK Size 6 Partridge double low water

TAG Fine oval silver tinsel

TAIL Golden pheasant crest and red hackle tip

BUTT Black floss

BODY Embossed silver tinsel and bright orange floss

RIB Fine oval silver tinsel

THROAT Natural guinea fowl

WING Dark brown squirrel tail

CHEEKS Jungle cock

HEAD Black

Garry Dog

HOOK Size 6 Partridge double low water

TAG Fine oval silver tinsel

TAIL Golden pheasant crest

BODY Black floss

RIB Fine oval silver tinsel

THROAT Bright blue guinea fowl

WING Yellow and red goat

HEAD Black

PARTRIDGE
LOW WATER
1990

Munro Killer

HOOK Size 6 Partridge double low water

TAG Fine oval gold tinsel

BODY Black floss

RIB Fine oval gold tinsel

THROAT Orange hackle fibers and bright blue guinea fowl

WING Yellow hackle and black squirrel tail

HEAD Black

Watson's Fancy

HOOK Size 6 Partridge double low water

TAG Fine oval silver tinsel

TAIL Golden pheasant crest

BODY Red floss and black floss

RIB Fine oval silver tinsel

THROAT Black cock hackle

WING Black squirrel tail

CHEEKS Jungle cock

HEAD Black

UNKNOWN
DEE DOUBLE
Late 1800s

BIBLIOGRAPHY

The books below are among the valuable resources for information on the history of the Atlantic salmon fly from the early nineteenth century to the present, and for fly dressings, instructions, and illustrations and photographs of patterns. For each publication, the first edition is listed. Also noted are reprints of especially significant books as well as later editions containing additional material of particular interest to the flytyer or researcher.

Alexander, Col. Sir James Edward. SALMON FISHING IN CANADA BY A RESIDENT. London: Longmans, Green, Longman and Roberts, 1860.

Anderson, Gary. ATLANTIC SALMON & THE FLY FISHERMAN. Montreal: Salar Publishing, 1985.

Atherton, John. THE FLY AND THE FISH. New York: MacMillan, 1951.

Bainbridge, George C. THE FLY-FISHER'S GUIDE. Liverpool, England: private printing, 1816.

Bates, Joseph D., Jr. THE ART OF THE ATLANTIC SALMON FLY. Boston: David R. Godine, 1987.

————. ATLANTIC SALMON FLIES & FISHING. Harrisburg, Pennsylvania: Stackpole, 1970.

Blacker, William. BLACKER'S ART OF ANGLING. London: private printing, 1842.

————. BLACKER'S ART OF FLY-MAKING. London: private printing, 1855.

————. BLACKER'S CATECHISM OF FLY-MAKING, ANGLING, AND DYEING. London: private printing, 1843.

Buckland, John, and Arthur Oglesby. A GUIDE TO SALMON FLIES. Ramsbury, England: Crowood, 1990.

Cholmondeley-Pennell, Harry. FISHING FOR SALMON AND TROUT. London: Longmans, Green, 1885.

Ephemera (Edward Fitzgibbon). THE BOOK OF THE SALMON. London: Longman, Brown, Green, and Longmans, 1850.

————. A HANDBOOK OF ANGLING. London: Longman, Brown, Green, and Longmans, 1847. (The second edition, 1848, and the third edition, 1853, contain flies and dressings not found in the first.)

Falkus, Hugh. SALMON FISHING, A PRACTICAL GUIDE. London: H. F. & G. Witherby, 1984.

Fisher, Major A.T. ROD AND RIVER. London: Richard Bentley, 1892.

Fisher, Paul (W. A. Chatto). THE ANGLER'S SOUVENIR. London: Charles Tilt, 1835.

Francis, Francis. A BOOK ON ANGLING. London: Longmans, Green, 1867. (The fourth edition, 1876, includes additional flies and dressings; the fifth, 1880, has a plate with three new flies; the seventh, 1920, revised by Sir Herbert Maxwell, replaces the handcolored plates with photographic plates.)

————. BY LAKE AND RIVER. London: Field Office, 1874.

Fulsher, Keith, and Charles Krom. HAIR-WING ATLANTIC SALMON FLIES. North Conway, New Hampshire: Fly Tyer, 1982.

Grey, Viscount of Fallodon. FLY FISHING. London: J. M. Dent, 1899.

Hale, J. H. HOW TO TIE SALMON FLIES. London: Sampson, Low, Marston, 1892. (The second edition, 1919, and the third edition, 1930, list 361 patterns, but do not include all of the 40 found in the first. The second and third incorporate most of the 345 patterns from John J. Hardy's SALMON FISHING.)

Hansard, George A. TROUT AND SALMON FISHING IN WALES. London: Longman, 1834.

Hardy, John J. SALMON FISHING. London: Country Life, 1907.

Herbert, Henry William. FRANK FORESTER'S FISH AND FISHING OF THE UNITED STATES AND BRITISH PROVINCES OF NORTH AMERICA. London: Richard Bentley, 1849.

Hewitt, Edward Ringwood. SECRETS OF THE SALMON. New York: Charles Scribner's, 1922.

Hi-Regan (J. Dunne). HOW AND WHERE TO FISH IN IRELAND, A HAND-GUIDE FOR ANGLERS. London: Sampson, Low, Marston, 1886.

Hodgson, W. Earl. SALMON FISHING. London: A. & C. Black, 1906.

Jorgensen, Poul. DRESSING FLIES FOR FRESH AND SALT WATER. Rockville Centre, New York: Freshet Press, 1973.

———. SALMON FLIES: THEIR CHARACTER, STYLE, AND DRESSING. Harrisburg, Pennsylvania: Stackpole, 1978.

Keene, J. Harrington. FLY-FISHING AND FLY-MAKING. New York: Orange Judd, 1887.

———. THE PRACTICAL FISHERMAN. London: "The Bazaar" Office, 1881.

Kelson, George M. THE SALMON FLY. London: Wymans, 1895. (Reprinted by Angler's and Shooter's Press, Goshen, Connecticut, 1979.)

———. TIPS. London: private printing, 1901.

Kirkbride, John. THE NORTHERN ANGLER. London and Carlisle: C. Thurnam, and London: Edwards & Tilt, 1837.

Knox, A. E. AUTUMNS ON THE SPEY. London: John Van Voorst, 1872.

La Branche, George M. L. THE SALMON AND THE DRY FLY. Boston and New York: Houghton Mifflin, 1924.

Mackenzie-Philips, Peter. SUCCESSFUL MODERN SALMON FLIES. London: Blanford Press, 1989.

Mackintosh, Alexander. THE DRIFFIELD ANGLER. Gainsborough, England: private printing, 1806.

Malone, E. J. IRISH TROUT AND SALMON FLIES. Gerrards Cross, England: Colin Smythe, 1984.

Marbury, Mary Orvis. FAVORITE FLIES AND THEIR HISTORIES. New York and Boston: Houghton Mifflin, 1892.

Maxwell, Sir Herbert. FISHING AT HOME AND ABROAD. London: London and Counties Press, 1913.

———. SALMON AND SEA TROUT. London: Lawrence and Bullen, 1898.

Morgan, Moc J. FLY PATTERNS FOR THE RIVERS AND LAKES OF WALES. Llandysul, Wales: Gomer, 1984.

Newland, Henry. THE ERNE, ITS LEGENDS AND ITS FLY FISHING. London: Chapman and Hall, 1851.

Norris, Thad. THE AMERICAN ANGLER'S BOOK. Philadelphia: E. H. Butler, 1864.

O'Gorman. THE PRACTICE OF ANGLING, PARTICULARLY AS REGARDS IRELAND. Dublin: Curry, 1845.

Phair, Charles. ATLANTIC SALMON FISHING. New York: Derrydale Press, 1937. (Reprinted by Premier Press, Camden, South Carolina, 1985.)

Pryce-Tannatt, T. E. HOW TO DRESS SALMON FLIES. London: A. & C. Black, 1914. (The third edition, 1977, and the 1987 reprint have additional patterns and plates.)

Roosevelt, Robert Barnwell. GAME FISH OF THE NORTHERN STATES OF AMERICA AND BRITISH PROVINCES. New York: Carleton, 1862. (Reprinted by Arno Press, New York, 1967.)

Sage, Dean. THE RESTIGOUCHE AND ITS SALMON FISHING. Edinburgh: David Douglas, 1888. (Reprinted by Angler's and Shooter's Press, Goshen, Connecticut, 1973.)

————, ed. SALMON AND TROUT. New York: MacMillan, 1902.

Sandeman, Fraser. ANGLING TRAVELS IN NORWAY. London: Chapman & Hall, 1895.

————. BY HOOK AND BY CROOK. London: Henry Sotheran, 1892.

Sawada, Ken. THE ART OF THE CLASSIC SALMON FLY. Tokyo: Kodansha, 1990.

Scrope, William. DAYS AND NIGHTS OF SALMON FISHING ON THE TWEED. London: Murray, 1843.

Stewart, Tom. TWO HUNDRED POPULAR FLIES. London: Ernest Benn, 1979.

Stoddard, Thomas Tod. THE ART OF ANGLING AS PRACTISED IN SCOTLAND. Edinburgh: Chambers, 1835.

Sturgis, William Bayard. FLY-TYING. London and New York: Charles Scribner's, 1940.

Taverner, Eric. FLY-TYING FOR SALMON. London: Seeley, Service, 1942.

————. SALMON FISHING. London: Seeley, Service, 1931.

Taylor, Samuel. ANGLING IN ALL ITS BRANCHES. London: Longman and Rees, 1800.

Tolfrey, Frederic. THE SPORTSMAN IN CANADA. London: T. C. Newby, 1845.

————, ed. JONES'S GUIDE TO NORWAY AND SALMON-FISHER'S POCKET COMPANION. London: Longman, Brown, Green, and Longman, 1848.

Waddington, Richard. SALMON FISHING: PHILOSOPHY AND PRACTICE. London: Faber and Faber, 1959.

Wade, Henry. HALCYON. London: Bell and Daldy, 1861.

Webster, David. THE ANGLER AND THE LOOP-ROD. Edinburgh and London: William Blackwood, 1885.

Wheatley, Hewett. THE ROD AND THE LINE. London: Longman, 1849.

Wulff, Lee. THE ATLANTIC SALMON. New York: A. S. Barnes, 1958. (A revised and augmented edition, Nick Lyons Books, New York, 1983, contains a new foreword, over fifty additional pages, and new photographs.)

Younger, John. ON RIVER ANGLING FOR SALMON AND TROUT. Edinburgh: William Blackwood, 1840.

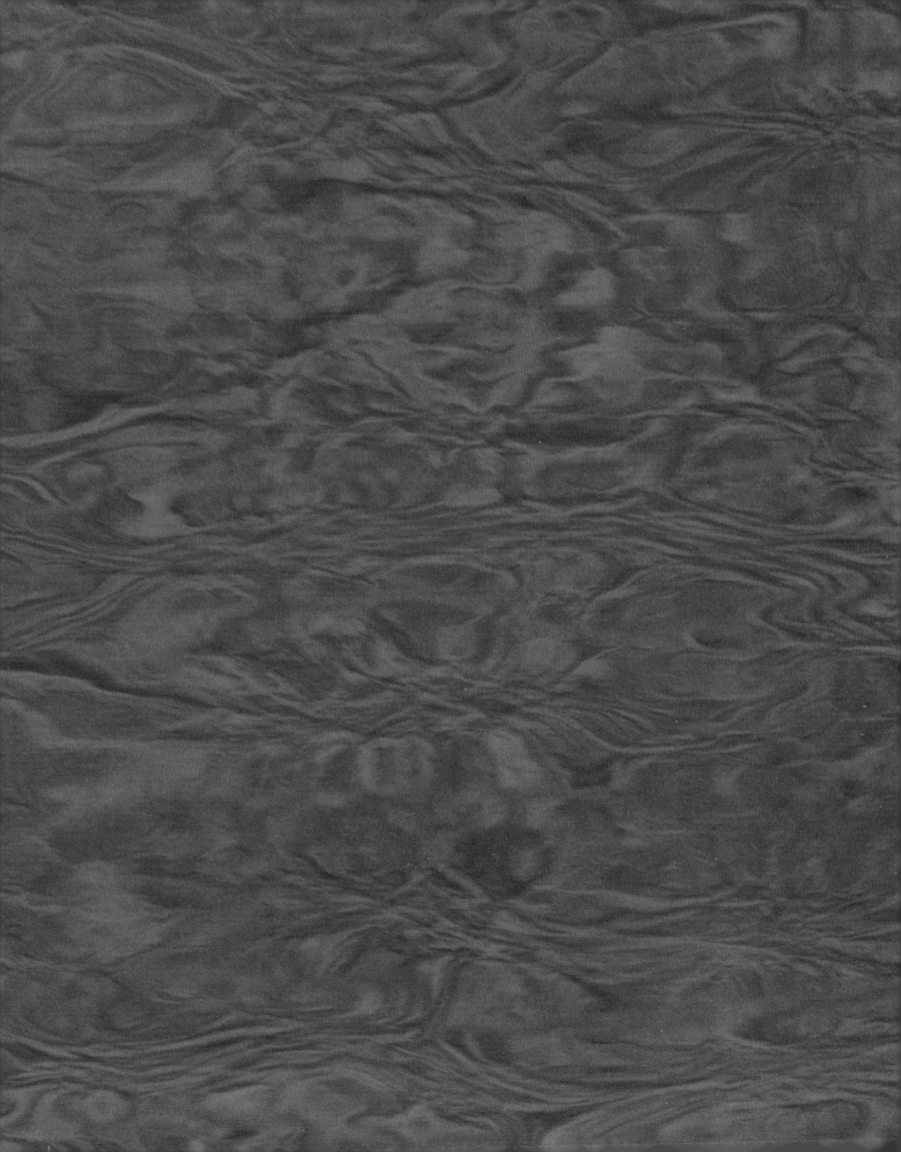